Journalism

Stories from the Real World

Journalism

Stories from
the Real World

Retta Blaney

editor

**NORTH
AMERICAN
PRESS**

Golden, Colorado

Book design by Deborah Rich
Cover photograph by Glenn J. Asakawa

Library of Congress Cataloging-in-Publication Data

Journalism : stories from the real world / Retta Blaney,
editor.
               p.   cm.
    ISBN 1-55591-935-9
    1. Journalism. 2. Journalists–United States–
    Biography.
  I. Blaney, Retta.
  PN4871.J68 1995
  070'.92'273–dc20
  [B]   95-44494
                                       CIP

Printed in the United States of America

0 9 8 7 6 5 4 3 2 1

North American Press
A division of Fulcrum Publishing
350 Indiana Street, Suite 350
Golden, Colorado 80401-5093

For my mother,
who has always believed

I love you, Mom

Contents

Acknowledgments   *xi*

Introduction, Walter Cronkite   *xiii*

One: **The Importance of Fact-checking, Accuracy, and Proofreading   1**

The *Other* Reunion Planning Business, *Randy Bobbitt*   2

When Even Triple-checking Isn't Enough, *J. Frazier Smith*   4

A Three-legged Woman?   *Don Black*   6

Back to Basics Counts in News Stories, *Harriette Bias Insignares*   8

A Lesson in Biological Differences, *Retta Blaney*   12

What Was for Sale?   *Robert N. Rothstein*   15

Two: **Questioning, Listening, Looking, and Speaking Up   17**

The Man Behind Alex Haley and *Roots,* *Fred A. Woodress*   19

Play Dumb and Act Smart, *Bruce E. Johansen*   21

Never Stop Listening, *Eileen Fredman Solomon*   23

Don't Expect to Always Be Liked, *Ruth Bayard Smith*   25

When a "Dumb" Question Leads to a Great Story, *Carole Rich*   28

When in Doubt, Ask!   *Tom Wheeler*   30

A Now-famous Answer to a Different Question, *Richard D. Smyser*   32

Three: Judgment   35

Out of Your Mind and onto Paper, *John Devaney*   36

Knowing What *Not* to Include, *Renée K. Gadoua*   38

Sometimes It Pays to Hold Back, *Wallace D. Beene*   42

Don't Write a Check with Your Mouth that Your Actions Can't Cash, *David H. Nimmer*   43

Never Can Say Goodbye, *Susan Ruel*   49

Four: Persistence   51

Going One-On-One with Reagan, *Bill Gruver*   52

Covering Jimmy *Who? Laurie O'Brien*   55

On Digging Deeper, *Ron Pruitt*   61

Doing the Legwork in Nicaragua, *Robin K. Andersen*   64

Criss-cross, *Peter Benjaminson*   68

Five: You Never Know Until You Try   70

A Conversation with Howard Hughes, *W. Parkman Rankin*   71

George C. Wallace, *David Dick*   73

Green Jelly Beans, *Emil Dansker*   80

"Stealing" the Stadium Plans, *Emil Dansker*   82

Go with Your Gut, *Gregg Hoffmann*   85

Six: Don't Let Yourself Be Used   87

Beware of the Overhelpful Source, *Ron Pruitt*   88

Even Pros Get Taken, *Edwin Diamond*   91

Joining the Women's Pages, *Don Corrigan*   94

A Cautionary Tale, *Joan H. Lowenstein*   98

Seven: Occupational Hazards   100

There's No Proof Like a Tape, *Sylvan Fox*   101

No Tapes, *Tom Wheeler*   105

My Date with Hugh Hefner, *Louise Montgomery*   107

First Day, *Peter Benjaminson*   111

Lost in Translation, *Tom Wheeler*   113

**Eight: Doing the Best Under
Difficult Circumstances   114**

Reporting in Dallas on that Fateful Day,
Jim Featherston   115

Covering a Kind of Coup in Buenos Aires,
J. Laurence Day   123

So What's Your First Question? *Tom Wheeler*   129

Reading Between the Lines,
Leonard R. Sussman   131

Nine: Covering Death   134

Wanting to Be There, *Michael Shapiro*   136

Death and the Lessons of Life, *Michael Sewell*   140

How Do You Feel About That? *Joann Lee*   145

RFK's Shooting, *James Bow*   148

Covering Sensitive Stories Accurately,
Richard D. Smyser   150

Ten: Ethics   153

An Act of Sheer Moral Cowardice,
Robert H. Russell   154

A Journalist's Camera Never Lies, *P. J. Corso*   156

How to Handle a Charlatan—and a Bribe,
Jim Pratt   159

Don't Get Too Caught Up in One Story,
Mike Ludlum   161

Campaign for Cuba, *Sandra H. Dickson*   165

Is "Balanced" Coverage Really Fair Coverage?
Robin K. Andersen   169

Power of the Press, *Maurine H. Beasley*   174

About the Author   175

Acknowledgments

I am one of the happiest people on earth to finally be able to hold this book in my hands. It has been a long struggle. Rejected outright by three agents, I was dumped by a fourth after a year. More publishers have said no to this book than I had known existed. But it has found its home, and a very good one at that, and now I have the opportunity to express my gratitude to those who made it possible:

To Walter Cronkite, who responded by return mail to my letter asking him to help me by writing the introduction. "I don't have time to labor over an adequate introduction right now, but I have enclosed a letter which might help you get the cooperation you require from the professors and a publisher," he wrote. "And, as you see, if it all comes about, I'll somehow find the time to do that introduction." You found the time and I am deeply grateful.

To my contributors, most of whom were strangers to me when this project began in 1992. You were willing to help an unknown editor with no publisher in sight. Your stories shine, and you have made "our" book so much stronger than I ever could have imagined. Thank you.

To Shirley Lambert at North American Press who saw potential in a book that kept falling through the cracks elsewhere. The academic presses had told me it was too commercial; the commercial presses told me it was too academic. Shirley said, "It's a great idea. We can work it out." And she did. A creative publisher looking for original work is a rare find. I'm glad I found one.

To Brian L. Steffens and Ed Avis for first publishing my essay in *Quill* in June 1992 and to Lisa Mock at the Society of Professional Journalists for her enthusiasm and for putting me in touch with some great contributors. The book is finally here!

To Sr. Maura Eichner of the College of Notre Dame of Maryland who taught me always to "hammer on doors with the heart. All occasions invite God's mercies and all times are his seasons."

To my family—Kate Kinney, Angie D'Agostino, Marie Warmbold, and Arthur Pais. Thank you for your love, prayers, and support. You have always been there for me.

To Mary Bloom who helps me live the questions, to Peri Murphy who helped me understand about the cycles of barrenness and fruitfulness and who kept me going by reminding me that fruitfulness comes to those who wait and are faithful, and to all of my family at the Cathedral of St. John the Divine. I don't know how I would have gotten through those traumatic months of autumn 1994 without your help. You showed this only child what it is like to be part of a large and caring family. Thank you.

Most of all I thank God for that wonderful, powerful, sustaining gift of hope. For a long time it seemed to me that rejection was the story of my life, but now I see that hope—not rejection—is the real story of my life.

Introduction

Journalists—that is, people who report, write, and edit for newspapers and broadcast—can't agree on what it is they do. Some, such as I, cling to the belief that ours is a profession. Others put themselves down as simply practicing a trade. Some practitioners degrade the occupation as a business, but I label them as cynics.

I defend journalism as a profession on the grounds that we practice an ethic. Our intention is to be factual and fair, and, indeed, on any responsible medium that is our mandate. That the ethic sometimes is honored more in the breach scarcely disqualifies us as a profession. If that were the criterion, neither lawyers nor doctors, as a class, would qualify.

In fact, it is the doctors and lawyers who are most critical of our assumption that we news people are professionals. They are likely to point out the stringent and lengthy education they endure and the certification that they must receive before practicing. If that were the only basis for judgment, the claim would stand that we journalists do not qualify.

Our education is not prescribed and there is no requirement in law that we prove our capabilities to practice. News people in doing their jobs offend a lot of people, particularly those who would prefer to do their business—mercantile, industrial, political, or what have you—in the dark, and some of them occasionally suggest that there should be a system of licensing journalists. We can thank our lucky stars that these suggestions immediately run afoul of our constitution's First Amendment protection of a free press and free speech. We can have neither if some appointed body has the power to choose who can speak or write.

This, however, does not excuse us from the responsibility to acquire at least some basic knowledge before setting forth in the news-gathering world. We meet this goal by many routes. Most, perhaps, get a formal education in journalism at university communication schools. Many concentrate their undergraduate years in general academic subjects and reserve their education in journalism for post-graduate studies. And many move into journalism directly from school without classroom instruction in how to report and write for print or put together a television newscast.

But regardless of the nature of their education, the fact is that few are hired by newspapers or broadcasters today without university degrees, and some of the more prestigious news institutions require advanced degrees.

This is a far cry from the journalism of my formative years as a newsman before World War II. There was no television then, of course, and radio was still in its infancy, but in city rooms around the country college graduates were a comparatively rare breed. Most of the reporters and rewrite men (few women on those desks!) were graduates only of the school of hard knocks—and a lot of experience.

Today's college graduates are only arguably a great improvement. They undoubtedly are far superior in handling the big stories reflecting our increasingly complex society, but there is some question whether their educational elitism hasn't separated them from the general populace in reporting the street stories that are the grist of most local news.

Whatever their backgrounds, those new reporters and writers of today still are cubs—wet behind the ears with a lot to learn from on-the-job training. To their great credit, the good journalism schools today try to fill their academic rolls with those who have "been there"—those who have served their time on newspapers or at broadcast facilities. This in an acknowledgment that, in journalism, no amount of book learning can prepare one for the hard lessons of practical experience. While this probably applies to many businesses and professions, journalists can only consider their education well rounded when they have learned to apply those ethics of accuracy and fairness under the duress of deadline pressure.

Those are the lessons to be learned at the feet of the old pros; that is, the old practitioners of the profession of journalism.

—*Walter Cronkite*

The Importance of Fact-checking, Accuracy, and Proofreading

The writers in this section learned the hard way that in journalism you've got to get it right. When you don't, it's embarrassing to you and your paper, and may even cost you your job.

Randy Bobbitt found out that the people providing you with information can't always be trusted. Take all the information they give you—but then check it out. The time it takes will be well worth the hassle it can save you. As Bobbitt points out, checking a fact doesn't have to take all that much time, so make it a habit.

Sometimes, though, even triple-checking isn't enough, as Frazier Smith discovered. He also trusted a source and got burned. He did all he could to verify the information, but his source obviously had a reason for leaking the tip to him. A reporter can't exist without sources, but a good reporter knows better than to rely on that source too much. Take the information, question why you are getting it, and then check the record. Then you've fulfilled your responsibility. Smith couldn't have known that the record was faulty, but at least he knew he had done his best to get it right.

Don Black, Harriette Bias Insignares and I learned the importance of using that one correct word—and getting every basic detail—in a journalism story. Every fact counts, no matter how small. To paraphrase scripture, if your editors can't trust you with the little details, how can they trust you with the big ones?

And if you don't check your copy and proofread to the nth degree, you will learn, as Robert Rothstein did, that sloppy journalists become unemployed journalists.

The *Other* Reunion Planning Business

Randy Bobbitt

I've always found it effective to use self-deprecating humor in telling students about some of my own professional screw-ups, and this is one that I use when trying to emphasize the importance of attribution and fact-checking.

I was writing a feature story for the *Tampa Tribune* about two young men who had started a small business that specialized in planning high school reunions in the Tampa Bay area.

When I asked one of the men if there were any similar companies in the area, he looked me squarely in the eye and said, "No, there are no others in the Tampa Bay area; the closest similar company is in Orlando."

He sounded so confident that I did not feel it necessary to verify it. Instead, I merely paraphrased and attributed the statement to him. I did not attribute it because I felt it might have been disputed; I did it out of habit. I usually interject here that attribution is sometimes more of a habit than it is a case of adhering to a set of rules.

The text of the story included the following sentence: "'The company is the only one of its kind in the Tampa Bay area,' Ferguson said, adding that his nearest competitor is in Orlando."

The morning the story ran, my editor called me at home. He was not happy. He had just received a call from a local woman who ran the *other* reunion planning business in Tampa. She had explained to my editor that the two companies had been bitter rivals for several years, engaging in name-calling and threatening legal action over customer referrals, advertising claims, and other competitive matters. My blunder added fuel to the fire.

My editor called the man who made the claim, but he denied he said it and insisted that I had misunderstood him.

I tell my students that the fact that I attributed the claim to him did not get me off the hook for the factual error, but at least I was sharing the responsibility with the person making the claim. It would have been substantially more troublesome if I had simply made the statement without attribution.

What was most embarrassing for me and the *Tribune* was that checking the man's claim would have been so simple: The Tampa Yellow Pages listed both companies under the category of "reunion planners." There was also a national association for such businesses, which I could have called for information.

My punishment: I had to apologize to the woman who ran the competing business and interview her—face-to-face—for a similar story. It was the toughest interview I've ever done. I also kept my handwritten notes from the first story for several years afterward in case their squabble ended up in court and I was called to testify.

This was the most embarrassing blunder I have made in fifteen years of freelance writing. To this day, I have never again made a factual error. I double-check everything. Luckily, no real harm was caused by my sloppiness. But it did make me a much more responsible journalist.

Randy Bobbitt is an assistant professor at the W. Page Pitt School of Journalism at Marshall University in Huntington, West Virginia.

When Even Triple-checking Isn't Enough

J. Frazier Smith

There is a saying among reporters and editors in many newsrooms: You haven't "arrived" until you've been sued.

Well, I "arrived" in 1984–85, when a lawsuit was filed against the *Cincinnati Enquirer* and me alleging defamation of character and invasion of privacy.

The story, which dealt with confirming that the Cincinnati Police Division had on its force an officer who had a juvenile criminal record, began with a ten-second phone call to me from an anonymous source.

Some months before the story appeared, the flamboyant president of the Fraternal Order of Police stood atop a parked police cruiser during a rally and proclaimed that the FOP was against being investigated by the city's Office of Municipal Investigation (OMI), a civilian body created to be a watchdog of the police. There had been some incidents involving white officers and African-American suspects and the use of deadly force.

What bothered the union president most was that OMI's chief investigator had been convicted of a felony as a youth. The investigator was an African-American male. The union president, from that same automobile platform, went on to say that the police division would never recruit, hire, and retain someone who had a criminal record.

That challenge, which aired over the city's three local TV news programs, touched off my "investigation" to prove or disprove the claim.

About two or three weeks after the public challenge, I received a phone call claiming that there was an officer within the ranks who had a juvenile record.

Months later (I can't recall exactly how many), after being furnished with the officer's name off the record and having his criminal record

4

confirmed on the record by a prison superintendent where the officer had served time, my story ran on Page 1.

My story, while built and buttressed with named sources that were used in the newspaper article, began with that one phone call from the source whose name remains a secret even today.

The officer, whom I telephoned a day or two before the story ran in an attempt to get him to comment on what I had found, filed suit much later after the story ran. His comment to me the night I telephoned him stays with me.

"Where did you get your information?" he asked.

"I can't tell you that," I answered.

"You will tell me—I promise you that," he responded.

With that brief exchange, I hung up the phone and swallowed hard.

The suit was settled out of court with the stipulation that my source would remain unnamed. My colleagues were happy that I had held my ground and not given up my source—a cardinal sin in journalism.

But there are some morals to my story, namely that my reporting and subsequent story caused the following to happen:

- It turned out that the officer's criminal record had been expunged by the courts, a fact unknown to the prison superintendent when he confirmed the officer's record. I found out later that a slip of paper that should have been with the officer's file was missing.

- Because the record had been expunged, the *Enquirer* was required to remove from its library any and all clips of the officer's arrest and conviction.

- Ironically, several years after my story and the lawsuit, the officer was dismissed from the police division after he kept money found in a purse or bag he and another officer had found while on duty. The money had been planted by the police division as part of a periodic morality check of its officers.

J. Frazier Smith, a wire editor at the Dayton Daily News, *was an assistant professor at Ohio University. He has worked at the* Cincinnati Enquirer *as metropolitan reporter, copy editor, and assistant metropolitan editor and has worked on the rewrite desk at* USA Today.

A Three-legged Woman?

Don Black

Iwas one of the few youngsters in this country who started at the bottom of a weekly newspaper and worked his way to the top. On the journey from "printer's devil" to daily newspaper editor I learned many lessons, one in particular about proper word usage.

My apprenticeship as an eighth grader in Hugoton, Kansas, began with sweeping floors and melting used type into pigs. Gradually I was graduated to plate casting, operating the flatbed press and later typing on the Linotype. In high school I shot and processed photographs for the newspaper.

But I was most proud of being a reporter. After attending college one year, I was graduated into writing stories.

During the summer one of those rare events for weekly newspapers happened. On a Wednesday afternoon, just hours before final press time, the sheriff's deputies reported a car accident in which a woman was injured.

Weekly newspapers seldom have spot news, so this was a "really big deal." And because it was near town and time was of essence, I got the assignment.

In my best cub reporter style I dashed out to the scene of the accident to learn that one woman in the two-car accident had broken her legs. I don't remember what happened to the other driver, but I knew I had a front page story.

I raced back to the newspaper and whipped up a credible story in time for the final press run. I did pretty well, so I was told by others.

The next Monday when my pride and head still were quite swollen, an old country correspondent complimented me on the story.

"But, what happened to that woman's third leg?" he asked.

6

Uh? What's that you say? What is this country bumpkin trying to pull over on me, a college kid, I asked myself.

"You wrote that she broke two of her legs," he explained. "That implies that she had three legs. If she had only two legs, you would have written that 'she broke both of her legs.'"

My ego tumbled. He was right and I knew it. I had goofed. Now as a journalism professor I tell my students that story to illustrate how important the right words are—and to protect their egos and their jobs.

Don E. Black, a former daily newspaper editor, teaches journalism at Western Illinois University in Macomb.

Back to Basics Counts
in News Stories

Harriette Bias Insignares

Even in news, it's the little things that count, and the by-word is never overlook the basics.

It was the "day after"—after writing the biggest story I had ever been assigned. I felt butterflies all the way to work.

Riding along I-75 into the heart of Atlanta, that Monday morning in 1985, it was all I could do to keep my mind on the road. I had done it. I had interviewed, for the better part of a Saturday afternoon, the Army's highest-ranking female general, Brigadier General Sharian Cadoria. This most engaging lady had been a bundle of all kinds of paradoxes, for a general that is, but I had managed to get the story.

As I stepped off the elevator at the *Atlanta Journal and Constitution* that Saturday afternoon, I could see two figures in military uniforms standing just inside the newsroom. My heart sank. Am I late? A glance at my watch confirmed that I was on time with ten minutes to spare. So I took courage and approached them to introduce myself. On checking with them about the time of our appointment, I learned that it was the general's habit to arrive thirty minutes ahead of time. I guess that's one way to move up the ranks and, no doubt, a logical outcome of war strategy and surprise attack.

Not really being late, I wasn't sure whether an apology was in order. But I was representing the newspaper, so I observed the necessary protocol. I decided in that very moment that I would never view time in the literal sense when dealing with the military. I'd arrive an hour ahead just to be safe.

And this is where the paradoxes began. Gen. Cadoria didn't bluster, complain, or assert her position. Instead she was most accommodating and generous with her answers and her time. She proved to be bright, witty, and entertaining, certainly not what the Gilbert and Sullivan play,

8

H.M.S. Pinafore would call "the very model of the modern major general." And therein arose my dilemma of how to best present her story to the public.

My editor had insisted that I approach the story from the angle of the "hard-hitting general." But after meeting her, it was quite apparent that the real story resided in the very opposite. It was her departure from the traditional behavior and demeanor of a general that caught my attention and would similarly engage our readers. I had expected to meet a woman at least six feet tall, with the square jaw, stiff posture, and ample stature that would make her look official, powerful and in command. You know, that swagger of impatient arrogance that goes with power and ego.

Instead General Cadoria stood about 5' 3" in her two-inch black pumps, probably no more than 110 pounds soaking wet, petite and shapely in her uniform that displayed nary a wrinkle despite the parching Atlanta summer heat. She especially enjoyed talking about her close ties to her mother and the Catholic Church. Even with all of her official responsibility, she was proud to reveal that she was a lay reader at her church.

This general was the picture of a ballet dancer, the belle of the ball, the society hostess. But looks were deceiving. When she opened her mouth, you quickly realized that this was a savvy lady, self-confident, with strong convictions about leadership, religion, family, success, and her future. Her assistant, a female captain, also got into the interview, saying that the general was such a success in leading people because she didn't bellow and throw her weight around. Instead she ruled with an iron hand in a kid glove.

Feeling quite comfortable about how the interview had gone, I couldn't wait to write this story. I told Atlanta readers what I thought was everything they'd want to know about this unique general: how she had stumbled into the military after being stopped in the hall in college and asked to sit in on a recruitment session just to swell the audience; how she had been decorated for service in Vietnam; how she had worked as a protocol officer in the White House; and how she was now headed to the Pentagon to become the first female director of manpower for the Joint Chiefs of Staff.

Of course, the story went through several editors' hands before it finally rolled off the presses. And I would soon see what I thought was my best story ever. However, despite all of the surprising, humorous, astounding, inspiring facts I included about her in the article, I entered the newsroom, not to the sound of compliments, thumbs up and high fives, but instead to a question yelled from the other side of the newsroom that hit

me like a cherry bomb rumbling in a fifty-gallon fuel can: BUT . . . HOW
. . . OLD . . . IS . . . SHE?

It was a little thing, seemingly insignificant in comparison to all her
accomplishments. Yet it counted because leaving it out of the article had
created a hole in the story and at least one dissatisfied reader. As I heard
the question, I could see my dreams of a Pulitzer Prize floating, at warp
speed, up, up and away into never-never land.

Despite my embarrassment and disappointment, there was something
good to save the day. In a few days, I received a letter from General Cadoria
thanking me for the story. She told me that someone from *PM Magazine*
in California had read the story and contacted her for a feature. She
added that someone from *Dollars and Sense* magazine had also read my
article and had nominated her to their list of the one hundred most prom-
ising persons to watch in the coming year. She flew to Texas to receive the
award. Just to think, my article, flawed though it was, had helped to advance the career of a military general.

I tell this story to students to emphasize some of the qualities of a good
reporter. There were three basic lessons I learned from this experience.
The first was that "on time" means different things to different people, so
a reporter should arrive well in advance of the appointment. It might be
a good idea to ask if the person anticipates running ahead of schedule or
behind.

The second lesson was that giving attention to details and routine facts
is just as important to the success of a story as the great achievements in a
person's life. The goal of the reporter is to answer the questions for readers that they would have asked if they could have covered the story. Questions left unanswered can create doubt and influence the reporter's credibility. Did he or she do a thorough job? Readers may be inclined to wonder whether other more important facts have been left out of the story.

Finally, the third lesson was that, try as they may, editors don't always
catch errors or notice missing elements. I have worked with interns in
the newsroom who would routinely send stories to the copy desk with
needless errors in spelling, grammar, etc., relying on the copy desk to
clean up the copy. Sometimes they awakened the next morning to find
their story peppered with errors in the paper. One copy editor told me
he actually did this to a lazy reporter to teach a lesson. Good reporters
care about the type of writing associated with their by-line. Therefore,
they get it right the first time because, even in news, it's the little things
that count.

Dr. Harriette Bias Insignares is Tennessee's Official State Poet and Arts Advocate. She has been a fellow with the American Society of Newspaper Editors, the American Press Institute and the Freedom Forum. Professor of journalism at Tennessee State University, she was the recipient of The New York Times *Fellowship in honor of Sylvia L. Wilson. She has worked for the* Tennessean, *the* Atlanta Journal and Constitution, *the* Gwinnett Daily News, *the* Nashville Pride, *and the* Metropolitan.

A Lesson in Biological Differences

Retta Blaney

I heard a news brief on the radio about some New York lawmakers who were trying to ban dwarf tossing. The item caught my attention for a reason beyond the obvious questions of why anyone would want to toss a dwarf and why it is legal to begin with. I get a particular kick out of dwarf stories because of a journalism lesson I learned years ago at the *Baltimore Sun*.

I was working the cop beat every night as a college intern in January 1978. I did the whole routine—checked out a *Sun* car, drove to the police stations and phoned in stories. I was about as gosh-by-golly as anyone who ever walked into the newsroom, so I was totally unprepared when Jay Spry, a perfectionist rewrite man, hung up on me my first night out because I didn't know how many engine companies had responded to a fire. (Studying Shakespeare and modern drama at the College of Notre Dame of Maryland had not prepared me for such questions, or such rudeness.)

After a couple of nights of that treatment I caught on. I saw a report about a very short man named Jimmy—the police report called him a midget—who had stolen somebody's ring on The Block, Baltimore's red light district. I knew it was offbeat enough to interest the city desk. I made sure I had everything—not just the whos, whats and wheres, but the cost of the ring, the size, what it looked like, etc. I didn't even care if Spry answered when I called in from the press room at police headquarters. This time I was ready for him—or so I thought. He listened to everything I said, then replied in his agonizingly slow, stuttering way: "Okay, okay, that's fine. Just one question. Is Jimmy a midget or a dwarf?"

I still wasn't totally used to Jay so I didn't catch on. I thought he just hadn't understood me. "I said he's a midget."

Spry: "How do you know?"

Me: "The police report said so."

Spry: "Well, you know, don't you, that there's a biological difference between a midget and a dwarf. You know that a midget is proportionally small, but a dwarf has a larger head. You know that, but the police may not. Go check it out." And he hung up.

I sat there dumbfounded. How could anyone think of such a question? I was too afraid of all the powers-that-be in the newsroom to just wait fifteen minutes and call back and say he was a midget, although I certainly didn't expect Jimmy to call the next day and ask for a correction, saying he was really a dwarf. I headed across the street to the Central District where the report was filed to ask the desk cop, wondering why I was doing something so stupid at eleven at night when everybody else I knew was comfortably at home.

I had hoped to just slip in and ask the first cop I saw and then slip back out. As luck would have it I got there at shift change and walked into a room full of blue uniformed macho maleness. Being the only woman, and an especially young and preppy one at that, it was difficult to slip in unnoticed. Slipping out unnoticed proved to be impossible.

I walked up to the first cop I saw and quietly asked my question. "Um, excuse me please, but there's this guy named Jimmy..."

"Oh yeah, hon, he stole somebody's ring on The Block tonight."

"Right, right, that's what I'm here about. Is Jimmy a midget or a dwarf?"

He looked at me with one of those below contempt expressions and asked with utter disgust: "What the hell's the difference?"

I patiently explained the biological distinction and said my editor needed to know. It was clear I had just made journalists hit an all-time low in his already low opinion. He couldn't believe that a bunch of college-educated people were spending the late night hours debating the semantics of what to call a very short person. He turned and shouted across the room, over that entire sea of blue uniforms: "Hey Sarge, the Sunpapers" (pointing to me) "wants to know if Jimmy's a midget or a dwarf."

Everyone in the room looked my way, laughed and called out some comment that showed their lack of appreciation for our profession. Sarge strutted across the room and asked me who the hell cared. I told him my editor did and told him why, because we certainly couldn't call someone a midget if he was really a dwarf. By this time cops had surrounded us; this was a new one, even for them. Then Sarge told me Jimmy was a midget. I was all set to go when someone piped in: "No Sarge, Jimmy's got a big head." Several others got into the act and they debated Jimmy's head size while I stood there wondering why I had ever thought it was so great to be a reporter.

Finally I broke into their discussion and asked for a consensus. Sarge told me to put him down as a midget. I thanked him and got out as fast as I could. I went back and called Jay and told him Jimmy really was a midget. He said that was fine, and then proceeded to go through the whole lecture again of how we couldn't call people midgets if they were really dwarfs.

I could have, quite happily. But not Jay Spry.

Now whether I'm teaching graduate feature writing or undergrad reporting, I always work in my midget-or-dwarf story. This has become not only one of the best stories I tell in class, but it has become a hit at parties as well.

Perhaps the legislators in New York should consider broadening their bill to include midgets. After all, if you can't toss a dwarf, you shouldn't be able to toss a midget either. Unless maybe those lawmakers don't know about the biological difference...

Retta Blaney has taught journalism at New York University, Brooklyn College, Marymount Manhattan College, and Montclair State University. She worked as a reporter for newspapers in New York and Maryland. Her freelance articles have appeared in the Washington Post, American Theatre, Crain's New York Business, *and other publications.*

What Was for Sale?

Robert N. Rothstein

It was 1951, and I was there when the worst typo of all time occurred. I was a reporter for the *Idaho Falls Post Register* in Idaho Falls, Idaho, after graduating with a major in journalism from the University of Colorado.

To appreciate what happened, you have to know the climate in Idaho Falls—Mormon, conservative, very straitlaced. This was the city where, when an erotic movie came to town, the women stood in front of the theater with umbrellas and beat any man who tried to enter.

And then it happened. To this day we don't know who made the mistake. Idaho Falls was one of the largest livestock auction markets in the country, and, after a particularly large sale, the *Post Register* ran a front page headline in 48-point type that screamed, "Ten Thousand Horses Sold Here." The only problem was somehow one of the "esses" got left off and the headline read, "Ten Thousand Hores Sold Here."

When the publisher discovered the error, he tried to recover the entire run from trains and newsstands, but it was too late. Within minutes, the story was all over the city, he was getting kidded at the Elks Club and, small town Colonel McCormick that he was, he fired anybody who had anything to do with the story—the proofreader, the Linotype operator and the reporter.

I had nothing to do with the error, and I escaped the ax, but the incident made me realize how fragile a newspaper career was. It was at this point that I decided to become a teacher.

Robert N. Rothstein, Ph.D., is a professor emeritus and former chairman of the faculty of communication at the University of Texas/Permian in Odessa. He has worked at the Brooklyn Eagle, *the* Denver Post, *and the* Idaho Falls Post Register *and is now a columnist at* Odessa American. *He is the author of* Anybody Can Write *and* Raising a Child on $5 Per Day.

Questioning, Listening, Looking, and Speaking Up

Usually when working on a story a reporter gains a source's respect—and gets information—by showing that person that he is prepared and knows a great deal about the subject they are discussing. In Fred Woodress's case, being prepared meant the difference between getting a good story or losing out entirely.

But occasionally it pays to act stupid, as Bruce Johansen learned. He figured out that the best way to get his source to talk to him was to act as if he didn't know what was going on. That way the source would let down his guard and, being the smart reporter he really was, Johansen got his story. What his reporting proved was that he wasn't dumb at all—he was taking in everything around him. He didn't just walk away, he got himself in there and then got what he needed. So don't be put off; there's more than one way to get a story.

Keeping alert during an interview also got Eileen Solomon a good scoop. She too found out that a good reporter can learn quite a lot when a source's guard is down. And she learned that it pays to keep listening.

It also pays to keep focused on getting your story, and not on pleasing your sources. Ruth Bayard Smith has had several reminders that you can't control people's reactions to your questions or stories, and you shouldn't try to. Reporters aren't in the business to write pleasing stories; they are in it to write fair and accurate stories.

One thing to remember when questioning a source is that you, the reporter, should be in charge of the interview. If you let a source intimidate you by belittling you or your questions (or by flattering you away from the subject), he, not you, will determine how the story turns out. This is something a reporter always needs to watch for.

Carole Rich, Tom Wheeler, and Richard Smyser kept their guards up, and overcame the shyness many new reporters have about asking questions. Rich and Wheeler learned the important lesson that it's better to have your source think you are stupid than to have your readers think so. A reporter's job is to get information; if you don't understand something, ask. Don't worry about dumb questions, even at press conferences. As Smyser says, you probably won't be the only one who's intimidated. And speaking up and asking questions could lead to surprising results.

The Man Behind Alex Haley and *Roots*

Fred A. Woodress

Very thorough research saved the day for me when I tried to record an oral interview with Alex Haley soon after David Wolper's dramatization of *Roots* had made television history as a miniseries on ABC-TV.

Alex Haley was on a college circuit speaking tour and was to arrive in Lexington to speak at the University of Kentucky. Working as a freelance writer at the time, I had obtained a tentative agreement from *Writer's Digest* to record an interview for their *Writer's Voice* series.

I pinpointed when Haley would arrive at a nearby Ramada Inn, and I waited in the lobby. He showed up, was very cordial, but told me I would have to check with his Hollywood attorney. He had signed a deal for an oral recording.

I went to the nearest pay phone, called his attorney long distance and was told no way would he agree to this interview, which would conflict with the contracted one.

There went my assignment and all the research work. In freelancing, time is money. Then I remembered reading the name of George Sims, a boyhood friend of Haley's who helped him research his writing. The pair had shared an apartment in New York when Haley first began freelancing after his retirement from the Coast Guard. Sims made his living handling gold ingots at the Federal Reserve in New York, doing his research at night and on weekends.

In desperation, I asked the motel clerk if Sims was registered. He was. It gave me a different interview than all of the others with Haley. I recorded the conversation. Towards the end of our interview, Haley joined us in the lobby and said some nice things about Sims, which added greatly to my profile of his researcher.

19

As it turned out, I got a good interview for print, but the quality of the recording was too poor for professional use. A hotel lobby is too noisy a place to record anything. The *Cincinnati Enquirer* liked my article so well that the editors featured it as the lead story in their Sunday magazine with an artist's sketch of Sims and Haley on the cover. The story was reprinted in the *Louisville Defender.*

That experience made me realize that the better a writer researches his subject, the better the interview will be. I would not have had an interview if I hadn't remembered an obscure mention of the name George Sims. Good research also enabled me to ask better questions.

I also learned to pick my locations carefully and to bring along a professional recording device when I planned to reproduce interview tapes.

Fred A. Woodress, Ed.D, APR, Fellow PRSA, retired in 1994 after teaching journalism at Ball State University for ten years. Besides teaching at BSU, Kentucky, and the U.S. Sports Academy, he has worked as a newsman on dailies in Missouri, Alabama, Kentucky, and Ohio and owned and operated a public relations-advertising business. He was chosen Outstanding Journalism Teacher in 1993 by the Society of Professional Journalists. He had a play published in Best One Act Plays 1948-49, *was one of the authors of the 87th Infantry Division military history, and wrote the books* Publicity Tips for Show People *and* Public Relations for Community/Junior Colleges.

Play Dumb and Act Smart

Bruce E. Johansen

This took place just after I graduated from the University of Washington with a B.A. (1972) and went to work at the *Seattle Times*. It was the fall of 1973, at the beginning of the oil shortages that hit the northwest rather hard. Since Washington State has no oil, some excitement occurred after an oil explorer announced that he was drilling for oil near a small town called Forks, on the western edge of the Olympic peninsula.

At this point, I usually draw a rough map on the board: "This is Seattle; this is Puget Sound, this is Mount Saint Helens. I got into my car and drove around the Sound, through Port Angeles, the small mill town in which I went to high school, then westward, to Forks." Forks is a very small town, so small that when my story noted that its streets had potholes, the town council passed a resolution calling me a liar.

The test well was a few miles south of town, along the highway. I approached the oil man who was running it at his motel room, and told him I was doing a piece for the *Seattle Times*. At this point, I usually ask if there is anyone in the room from Texas, because I am about to say some things about Texans. This guy was a New Mexican, but he filled the Texas oilman stereotype perfectly—big, smelly and arrogant. He looked me in the eye and said: "I don't like the press. And I don't like *you,* because you can't hardly talk." The truth is that I stutter. The oilman said: "I don't think you're playing with a full deck."

I went back to my car and tried to figure out how I would get the story. The best tactic, I decided, was to make myself out to be exactly what the oilman thought I was, a dumb kid who was not playing with a full deck.

So, I walked back to his motel room, slung my head to one side, slurred my speech, and asked the oilman if he would show me his "big, beautiful

21

rig." He was more than happy to do so, as he put his arm around my shoulder ("As if I were his dog," I sometimes say) and led me to his exploratory well.

It was a beautiful early fall day—fleecy clouds skidding across a turquoise sky. The oilman was very proud of his rig. I show students a photo of it and relate how he described it: "I put the American flag up there (at the top) myself. I painted it bright silver!?" I was interested, of course, in what he had found with the well, but he wouldn't answer any questions. Instead, as his eyes arched skyward, I found drilling charts on a shed beside the well which answered all my questions, and more. I scribbled notes until he was ready to leave, and then bid the oilman good day in my less-than-full-deck manner. He had no idea that I had read his charts.

I drove back to Seattle and wrote the story, which appeared under color art on a Sunday front page. At 8:30 A.M. Monday, I got a phone call from the oilman. He asked me where I had gotten all that information. "Read the charts on the wall," I said, and I would have given a week's pay to have seen the look on his face.

Bruce E. Johansen is a professor of communications and Native American studies at the University of Nebraska, Omaha. He is the author of Forgotten Founders: Benjamin Franklin, the Iroquois and the Rationale for the American Revolution, *and* Exemplar of Liberty: Native America and the Evolution of Democracy.

Never Stop Listening

Eileen Fredman Solomon

Sometimes I find myself listening to bits of other people's conversations. It reminds me that though my mother has often accused me of being her nosiest child, it has helped me make a living.

In the early 1980s, President Reagan was in St. Louis talking to some downtown group. I was working as an executive producer at KMOX-TV (now KMOV), then a CBS O & O. Our anchor had managed to land an exclusive one-on-one interview with the president, and the newsroom was quite busy.

The arrangements were that we would feed the entire interview back to the station live, then decide whether to air it all or to edit it down. As it was wrapping up, we decided to turn the whole thing around and run it in its entirety.

While the technical stuff was being worked out, I absent-mindedly watched our anchorman chat with the president. They were taking some publicity stills, but the mikes were still live and the tapes were still rolling. Our anchor mentioned that he knew Ed Rollins, who was working for the president, from his days at Washington University in St. Louis. Mr. Reagan then said something about how the White House was sorry to be seeing another Washington University associate leave.

Murray Weidenbaum, an economics professor from Washington University, was then the chief of the office of economic advisors in Washington. I knew this because we had done a series on the influence of this St. Louisan on the Reagan economic policy. If Weidenbaum was leaving, this was the first I—or, as it turned out, anyone—had heard of it.

We checked the tape, and then started making phone calls. The White House denied that Weidenbaum was leaving and said we had misunderstood the president. We called Weidenbaum in Washington, somehow got disconnected, and within minutes found that his phone number had been changed.

After a couple of hours, the White House announced that Weidenbaum was stepping down, in what turned out to be the first of several defections in the economic team.

They gave us the story first and when the story crossed as an urgent on the AP, it was credited to KMOX. I still have the wire somewhere.

I always tell this story in my basic reporting class. I use it to emphasize two points. First, it illustrates the importance of observation or, as my mother would say, nosiness. I tell the students to listen to everything, and to remember that the most important and revealing facts may come out of an interview subject's mouth when you least expect it. Second, I use the story to point out how power works. It is a small point in the scheme of things, but the fact that Weidenbaum's phone number was changed within minutes of our call impressed the heck out of me.

Eileen Fredman Solomon teaches broadcast journalism at Webster University in St. Louis, and has taught in the communications department at Lindenwood College in St. Charles, MO. She has worked as a writer, producer, and executive producer at television stations in St. Louis, Baltimore, and Tucson.

Don't Expect to Always Be Liked

Ruth Bayard Smith

My students bear all the worries of beginning reporters: How can they ask questions that might offend? How can they go where they may not be welcome? And what can they do to assure that their subjects will like their stories (and consequently them)?

Through experience they seem to become more comfortable getting information and access. But it seems to take them much longer to stop being paralyzed by potential reaction.

Early on in my classes, students are indoctrinated with the lesson that they're not doing PR for the subject or the cause at hand. I also stress that while they need to be sensitive to their subjects' feelings and concerns, they shouldn't censor themselves from asking certain questions.

My ultimate goal is that journalism students come to appreciate the unique aspect of the reporter-subject relationship and realize that worrying about a subject's reaction is futile because they can't predict when and how it will occur. In that vein, I usually share the following experiences:

- It was Barney Frank's congressional campaign and a gerrymandered district had pitted him against Republican incumbent, Margaret Heckler. Frank had buit an extensive coalition of disparate groups and pulled off a significant victory over the popular Mrs. Heckler. On election night I covered the win as a stringer for *Newsweek,* and in the question session, I asked which group he believed put him over the top. I fully expected a boilerplate answer, mentioning some of his supporters' affiliations. Instead he snapped, "That is the stupidest question I have ever been asked." I wish I could report that I insisted he still answer the question; rather, I stood stunned, as the proceedings were broadcast on live television.

- The Boston suburbs were in the throes of condominium conversion, and throughout the area tenants were being asked to vacate their apartments or buy their units. For a trend story for the *Boston Globe*, I visited with an elderly man and his wife who had just moved; they spoke passionately against the landlords, the management company, and the fates that put them in such a difficult position.
I was concerned for my subjects. They were not well and I worried about how the trauma would affect their respective heart conditions. I wrote a sympathetic piece that led with the couple's plight and included the following paragraph: "The Fitzgeralds had the option to stay and pay $90 more a month in rent or to purchase the unit at a reduced rate. But Tom Fitzgerald, 74, says, 'Sure I could have taken out a mortgage, but I would have been one hundred four when it ran out.' His wife [Margaret], 72, adds, 'I really feel sorry for the old people in the building.'"
I was sure they would feel vindicated, pleased that I put the phenomenon under scrutiny. Instead, I came home to hear Mr. Fitzgerald screaming on a phone message (somehow he had gotten my home number). He ranted and raved—so violently that I was sure he'd be subjected to the heart problems I tried to spare him.

- Newly arrived in Ann Arbor and teaching at the University of Michigan, I was asked by the *Detroit News* to write a piece for *MICHIGAN,* its Sunday magazine, defining the so-called "compass campuses" of the state college system. I was to visit each school for several days and give a sense of its character.
Located in the Upper Peninsula in Marquette, Northern Michigan University boasted a curriculum and programs that were quite impressive. Its staff was also kind and accommodating.
In fact, the section on Northern Michigan was one of the easiest to write; my subjects all spoke of the campus's

remote, often bitterly cold location, but added that they believed the school could rival many other more prestigious institutions.

I wrote about some of the school's more distinctive aspects, but began its description with a very real reference to the physical setting:

"As one student wryly understates, 'You don't come to Northern if you don't like the winter.'

'Or if you like to go to the mall and hang out,' adds another."

I also quoted a sophomore as saying, "You get to know the schedule of the ore ships (traveling Lake Superior). When you look forward to sitting and watching the ore being loaded, that doesn't say much about the entertainment here."

After the piece ran, the magazine was deluged with letters from people asserting that Marquette did, in fact, have a thriving—albeit small—mall and accused me of being a big city reporter who looked down on wholesome activities such as watching the ore ships.

In each instance, I certainly meant no malice. In fact, I tended to be sympathetic and tried to be so while remaining objective. The passionate responses against the pieces (and, in Congressman Frank's case, against my question) came when I least expected them.

My advice to students echoes that of a *Boston Globe* editor who years ago told me repeatedly (almost daily, as I recall) that I was not in the business to have people like me, that the goal of journalism was not to have the subject approve of the story wholeheartedly, and that if he did, I had not done a thorough job.

Ruth Bayard Smith is assistant professor of journalism at Montclair State University in Upper Montclair, NJ; she writes frequently about education, the media, and journalism history. Her work has been published in the Boston Globe, The New York Times, Folio, *and other local and national publications.*

When a "Dumb" Question Leads to a Great Story

Carole Rich

The old journalism cliché says there are no dumb questions, only dumb answers. Nonsense. There are dumb questions. But some of them can lead to great stories.

I was a cub reporter for the former *Philadelphia Bulletin*. I was assigned to cover a meeting of the Philadelphia School Board because the regular education reporter was ill. I knew nothing about the school board.

Shortly after the meeting began, the board passed the consent agenda, a group of items routinely passed without discussion because board members had previously discussed them or because the items were considered insignificant. But a little item on the consent agenda caught my eye.

The item said: Approves token losses of $30,000.

I was confused. I didn't think $30,000 should be considered "token."

After the meeting I went up to a school official and asked: "How could $30,000 be considered token losses?"

The school official rolled his eyes as if to say, "Spare me from this dumb new reporter." Then he snapped: "It's not token losses, it's losses of tokens."

Bus tokens.

The Philadelphia school district didn't provide the usual free school bus service for students at its 256 schools. The district sold students bus tokens for the city's public transportations system.

I was still confused.

"How could you lose $30,000 worth of tokens?" I asked.

The school official was getting annoyed.

"It happens every year," he said.

He mumbled something and told me to check with the school district's auditor if I wanted more information.

28

I did.

The auditor said there was a major theft at one of the schools that year, and he was investigating it. He said each school assigned a secretary or someone to sell bus tokens, but the procedure varied from one school to another. He seemed disturbed that there was no uniform policy to regulate how the tokens were sold, but he didn't want to be quoted about that. He supplied me with facts and figures about losses for the past few years and praised me for my curiosity and initiative.

I returned to the newspaper and told my editor about the tokens, the only item that really interested me in what seemed like an otherwise boring meeting.

"Write it," he said. And he told me to put the rest of the board's news in a separate story.

The next morning, I awoke to find my token story stripped across the front page. And the next day the school board announced that it would devise a uniform policy for selling the tokens at all its schools. After that, I was assigned to cover the education beat, one of the best beats on any newspaper.

Now I teach journalism at the University of Kansas. And I always tell my students about my "dumb" experience.

I also tell them it's better to feel dumb during an interview than afterward when you can't tell your readers something in your story because you were afraid to ask. Perhaps a big story will come from a "token" question.

Carole Rich is a professor at the William Allen White School of Journalism and Mass Communication at the University of Kansas. She has worked for the Philadelphia Bulletin, *the* Fort Lauderdale News/Sun-Sentinel, *and the* Hartford Courant. *She is the author of a journalism textbook,* Writing and Reporting News: A Coaching Method.

When in Doubt, Ask!

Tom Wheeler

My first interview was with the Man, the King Of The Blues, B. B. King himself. As I made my way across the cavernous lobby of the Las Vegas Hilton, I tried to picture what our meeting would be like— probably in a tiny sanctum with no distractions. I felt prepared, but boy, was I nervous. After the guard waved me through, I wiped the sweat from my nose, tried to calm my jitters, and then stepped into a pulsating back-stage suite larger than some nightclubs. Two dozen people were sipping drinks and chatting, most of them B. B.'s family members or old friends from Mississippi. They were all dressed better than I was and seemed utterly relaxed. I stuck out like Dolly Parton in an Amish church. Did they all turn in unison to stare at the flustered intruder, or did I just imagine it?

Suddenly woozy, I pictured myself tagging along behind my interviewee and pestering him as he tried to attend to his duties as host and star attraction. But B. B. surprised me by hushing the crowd and announcing the interview, adding, "Maybe you'll learn something about me you didn't know before." He had ordered sandwiches and more drinks and arranged for folding chairs. If I hadn't felt self-conscious enough already, I now found myself at the center of a catered event, conducting my first interview before seated, attentive observers who knew my subject in ways I never could.

At one point B. B. said, "My people were ashamed of the blues." I kept smiling and nodding like I had an inkling of what he was talking about. African-Americans ashamed of the blues? Wait a minute. They *invented* the blues. Pretending to listen, I started perspiring and wondered whether to stop the conversation and confess that I didn't get it. I thought, what's the worst that can happen? Well, I answered, I can make a fool of myself and prove to the multitude that I am a clueless geek who doesn't belong here.

30

But I took the plunge and admitted that he had lost me, and the King Of The Blues, as gracious as he is gifted, explained that in his youth, blacks were made to feel inferior by a complex web of stigmas and stresses. If performers sounded "white"—like Nat King Cole, say—that was good. But if they sounded "black," well, that was something to sweep under the rug. And the blues was the blackest music anyone had ever heard. As a young man, he had played the blues, all right, but he did it "behind closed doors, after twelve." I set my prepared questions on the floor and steered the conversation toward a topic I hadn't planned to cover, the relationships between race and music. It was the most fascinating part of any interview I've ever done.

No matter how hard we prepare for interviews, we must be ready for unforeseen twists and turns, and that the best exchanges usually result not from planned questions, but from careful listening and responding to the interviewee. And if something doesn't seem clear during the interview, it's not going to get any clearer when we go home and review the tape. Even in a high-pressured interview it's okay to say, excuse me, but I don't understand. Getting the goods is more important than looking cool.

Tom Wheeler is the author of The Guitar Book *and* American Guitars *(both Harper & Row) and the former editor of* Guitar Player *magazine. He is an associate professor at the School of Journalism and Communication at the University of Oregon, where in 1993 he won the Marshall Award for innovative teaching.*

A Now-famous Answer
to a Different Question

Richard D. Smyser

Good reporters aren't shy about asking questions, I tell my students. Good reporters especially aren't shy about asking questions at press conferences. I tell them because I remember being shy myself about asking questions, and especially at press conferences. But I got over it.

"I once asked a question at a press conference and the answer made history," I say. They perk up and then one of them most always asks, "Like what?"

"I once asked a president a question and he answered, 'I am not a crook.'"

(Pause. Reaction.)

"You mean Nixon?"

"I mean Nixon."

"What was the question?"

"'Mr. President, are you a crook?'"

(Sure laugh.)

Then I back off a bit.

It was November 17, 1973, at Disney World in Orlando, Florida, a time when the Watergate scandal was at one of its boiling points. President Nixon came to the annual convention of the Associated Press Managing Editors Association for an unusual Saturday night prime time nationally televised press conference.

John Quinn, vice president/news for Gannett Newspapers and APME president that year, had negotiated the Nixon appearance. Quinn decided to try something different—something that might keep the APME press conference more orderly—not so much shouting and popping up and down as was the case at stormy White House press conferences of

32

those times. Questions, he decided, would be restricted to APME members. Officers and directors would get preference in a prescribed order. The Washington press corps would, of course, come with the president, but they would be shunted off to one side. Some said Nixon was pleased with this arrangement, figuring he'd likely get more friendly questions from the grassroots editors.

As an officer myself of APME that year, I was in line to be a questioner. I had debated between two possible questions, but when my turn came I asked about a speech made just a short time before by Senator Mark Hatfield. There had been much discussion about the office of the presidency. Was it becoming unmanageable? Senator Hatfield had commented that no one person should be expected to shoulder so much responsibility without sharing some of it with the public.

Quoting the Oregon Republican senator, I asked, "Mr. President, do you think that this explains possibly how something like Watergate can occur?"

Yes, the president answered, that might be part of the reason. The year 1972, when the Watergate burglary occurred, had been a busy one for him. He'd visited China on the historic trip that led to the opening of diplomatic relations with the Communist regime. He'd been to Moscow where he had negotiated the first limited nuclear ban on defensive weapons. He didn't pay as much attention as he should have to his reelection campaign. However, "if mistakes are made, I am not blaming people down below. The man at the top has got to take the heat for all of them," he said.

Then, looking down at Harry Rosenfeld of the *Washington Post*, who was about to ask the next question, the president said, "Let me respond, if I could sir, before going to your question—since the question was raised about my tax payments."

Just before my question, Joe Ungaro, of the *Providence Evening Bulletin and Journal*, had cited the president's income tax payments of only $792 in 1970 and $878 in 1971. Were these figures correct and what were the president's views on elected officials disclosing their personal finances, Ungaro had asked.

Nixon had originally responded to Ungaro that those figures might be correct, but for those two years he had been granted a $500,000 tax exemption for donating his vice-presidential papers to the government, something President Lyndon Johnson had advised him to do. Now in addition to his response to my question about Senator Hatfield's speech, he wanted to say something more about the tax payments.

And then he went on and on and got deeper and deeper into his personal finances and then, concluding, "I welcome this kind of examination because people have got to know whether or not their president is a crook. Well, I am not a crook. I have earned everything I have got."

So, I concede to my students, it was really Joe Ungaro's question much more than mine to which the president was responding, but if you look at the transcript of the press conference you see my question and then Nixon's long response ending with the now historic line. So maybe I should get credit for at least an assist?

They usually agree and I make my point one more time: "Stand up and ask those questions, sweaty palms (which I still get sometimes) and all. You never know when Andy Warhol's 'fifteen minutes of fame' will come to you."

Richard D. Smyser has taught at the University of Tennessee, the University of Alaska, Anchorage, the University of Nebraska, Lincoln, and Pennsylvania State University. He has worked for the Chester (PA) Times *and the* Oak Ridger, *and has been active in national newspaper organizations.*

chapter three

Judgment

Good judgment is one of the most important qualities a reporter can have, but it is also one of the most elusive. The problem is that what applies in one situation may not in another. Developing good judgment is a lifelong task. When no fixed rules can be called upon, only sound judgment will save the day.

John Devaney and Renée Gadoua had to make a decision about what to include in a story. While they both chose to leave something out, his choice was wrong and hers was right.

But holding back doesn't always apply just to what is written. Sometimes, as Wally Beene learned, it applies to reporting as well.

David Nimmer experienced what may be the toughest judgment call of all—deciding when to grant anonymity to a source. He explains why it is important to hesitate before making a promise you may not be able to keep.

And then there are the times when your best judgment tells you to just give up. That's what Susan Ruel had to do, although not without a fight.

Out of Your Mind and onto Paper

John Devaney

For much of two weeks during the early 1970s, I was practically living side by side with Pete Rose, one of baseball's best hitters and most colorful personalities. It was during the off-season in Cincinnati, where he lived, and I followed Pete into his off-season haunts, usually places where people like him—"I would have carried a lunch pail if it wasn't for baseball," he told me—hung out. One of the places was a racetrack, River Downs, if I recall correctly.

At the track I watched Pete bet on horses heavily and rarely profitably. I asked him whether it was legally okay for a baseball player to be betting on sports, and he assured me that it was. I remember making notes something like this: "Betting fascinates Rose, because it is another form of competition, and if he is anything, he is a competitive animal." But when the time came to write the story, it seemed to me that the scenes at the racetrack did not fit neatly into a story that would appear in the magazine *Sport* during baseball season, so I dropped the racetrack scenes.

Some fifteen years later, when all those stories came out about Pete betting on anything in sight, including—according to some allegations— baseball games, I did more than a little self-booting in the rear and asked myself: Would your inclusion of the scenes of Pete betting so avidly in the 1970s have created more of a sensation than you realized? And would the resulting clamor have given me a journalistic beat, sold magazines, and alerted Pete and baseball to a dangerous situation, one that cost him his baseball career?

In reporting, I believe, a writer must always be thinking First Things First (most important stuff up front). I think I forgot the rule here. The fact that the betting scenes fit into the overall piece like a sore thumb caused me to forget that the sore thumb was the most important thing I

36

had. I have never forgotten those racetrack scenes while I have long since forgotten the scenes I used.

Moral, if there is one: If you can't shake something about a story out of your mind as you write, maybe you should take it out of your mind and put it on paper.

John Devaney taught journalism at Fordham University from 1980 until his death in 1994. He had been the sports editor of magazines at Fawcett Publications and CBS Publications, and sports editor at Parade *magazine. He wrote more than eighty nonfiction books, among them* Murder in the Harlem Mosque, Douglas MacArthur, Something of a Hero, *and* The History of the Indianapolis 500.

Knowing What *Not* to Include

Renée K. Gadoua

The freelance assignment came over the phone: Write a profile of Ellen Tarry, an eighty-eight-year-old African-American writer and activist. I'd never heard of her. David Scott, my editor, said Tarry converted to Catholicism in the 1920s and was a fringe member of the Harlem Renaissance. David told me to take my time.

The research started slowly. First I got a copy of Tarry's autobiography, *The Third Door.* Meanwhile, I headed to the library to dig up copies of her work. Tarry, according to one short biography in a reference book, was considered a pioneer for her use of black children as main characters in children's books. I asked a local librarian to search for copies for me. After nearly two months, she found a battered copy of *My Dog Rinty,* published in 1946. I also tracked down articles Tarry wrote during the 1930s and 1940s for religious publications such as *Commonweal* and the *Catholic World* and an early black newspaper, the *Amsterdam News.* And I found references to her in several books about the Harlem Renaissance.

As my notes piled up, a fascinating story began to emerge. Ellen Tarry was born in Birmingham, Alabama, and was raised a Congregationalist. Her parents, both of mixed blood, sent her to a Catholic boarding school in Virginia, sparking an interest in Roman Catholicism that led to her conversion and baptism in 1922 at the age of seventeen.

During Tarry's career as a journalist, her writings frequently decried injustice and segregation. She later moved to New York City, where she found herself in the midst of the Harlem Renaissance, the revival of black culture and literature. Among her friends were the celebrated poets Claude McKay and Langston Hughes.

Tarry also became involved in early efforts of the American Catholic Church to address segregation and racism. Other details made the story more compelling. Despite the racial discrimination she experienced, the light-skinned Tarry refused to "pass for white." Tarry's autobiography also mentioned, briefly, a yearlong marriage to a soldier and the birth of her daughter, Elizabeth.

My story was shaping up, even before I took an Amtrak train to New York City to interview Ellen Tarry. I spent an afternoon talking to the energetic octogenarian and filled a notebook with quotes and observations. I had expected her to spare an hour—two at the most—to talk to me. Instead, the interview lasted all afternoon and included poring over scrapbooks and family pictures.

Back home in Syracuse, I talked to scholars who traced Tarry's importance to the literary and religious worlds. I found one professor of literature who used Tarry's autobiography as required reading in one of her courses. I interviewed Tarry's colleagues, past and present.

No question about it, I had done my homework. Despite the piles of notes and clippings overtaking my office, though, I couldn't shake the feeling that I still didn't have enough to write a profile of this woman. So I added a few more calls to learn about her current role in her local church. I wanted some anecdotes to humanize the story and hoped to find a touching memory that would round out my research.

Several calls—most to Tarry's friends and colleagues who were in their seventies and eighties—resulted in perfunctory compliments. But I couldn't seem to find the one anecdote I was convinced would tie the story together. Finally, at the tail end of what I decided was to be my final interview, my source, Wally Roebuck, mentioned a friend who met his wife during a USO dance in 1943. Ellen Tarry, he said, had introduced the couple.

Jackpot!

"Mr. Roebuck," I said, barely able to contain my luck at stumbling upon this tidbit, "can you tell me how to contact your friend? I'd like to interview him about his memories of Miss Tarry."

It turned out they weren't *close* friends, but the guy's name was "John Novack, or Nowack, and he goes to St. Mark the Evangelist over on 138th Street."

"Do you by any chance have a phone number?" I asked.

No such luck. He had an unlisted phone number, Roebuck said.

"Well," I persisted, "do you have an address?"

He wasn't sure, but he thought John lived on St. Nicholas Avenue.

That meant nothing to a Central New Yorker like me, but I thanked him and hung up.

Although I had plenty of material for the story, I was sure that interviewing Novack, or Nowack, was the key to the article. The anecdote, I decided, was the perfect lead. It would highlight Tarry's personal impact and reveal a different side of her.

So I tried directory assistance. No luck. The phone company had no listing at that street under either spelling. Next I called the post office for the street's zip code. "What have I got to lose," I thought, as I wrote a short note to Mr. Novack. I guessed at the spelling of his name and addressed the note to St. Nicholas Avenue. I figured I could start organizing my notes and outline the story as I waited for a response.

I didn't wait long. Within four days John Novak responded with a handwritten letter, several color photographs, and some clippings that mention him. His phone number, it turned out, was listed under his second wife's maiden name. He urged me to call. "I will be glad to cooperate in your research," he wrote in spidery, blue handwriting.

When I called, he picked up the phone right away, as if he'd been waiting for me. I hardly had to ask any questions before he started recounting the night he met his wife, Geraldine. "I can remember how she was dressed—lacy sleeves and everything," he said. He remembered Father Smith who urged him to go to the dance "to meet some respectable ladies." He remembered the music, and the dancing, and meeting Ellen Tarry, with whom he had exchanged Christmas cards for many years. Did he appreciate Tarry's matchmaking? "Oh, yes," he said, laughing. "It was a trap and I was the cheese. It worked out. We were happy forty-five years."

After about fifteen minutes, Mr. Novak said he was tired and had to rest. I thanked him, hung up and turned to my computer to begin weaving this interview into my story. He had provided lots of details and a great narrative. The story was touching and romantic. It had a light touch, yet it set the scene because of its historic context. How could it go wrong?

But as I thought about the story and worked on it and read and reread my early draft, I knew it didn't work. The problem, I quickly realized, was that despite Novak's cute anecdotes and lively quotes, it just didn't fit. The tone was different from the rest of the research. Most of the story focused on her activism and her literary work. I never mentioned her stint working for the USO, and introducing the anecdote only muddied the chronology. Novak knew little about the rest of her career, and my short interview failed to make the link between different aspects of her life.

So, with some regret, I cut the anecdote from my story and rewrote the lead. But all was not lost. I had learned, again, that researching a complicated story takes time and often involves some deadends. I realized that I could try the same strategy—a letter with a vague address—to track down other sources. I remembered that it's always worth extra work to find a quote or detail that may advance a story or shed light on a person you're researching. I also realized that knowing what *not* to include in a story is just as important as knowing what to include. Sometimes, I learned, an interesting, lively anecdote fails to help a story.

Soon after my story on Ellen Tarry was published, I cleaned out my files and organized my notes. I almost threw away the note and pictures John Novak had sent me. Instead, I put them in my "Ideas" file. Maybe I'll do a story on World War II vets someday. I already have one source—and I know exactly how to contact him.

Renée K. Gadoua is a copy editor and reporter for the Syracuse newspapers. She has written on religious issues for several publications, including the Catholic Sun *and* Our Sunday Visitor. *A magna cum laude graduate of Le Moyne College, she earned a master's degree in magazine journalism from the S. I. Newhouse School of Public Communications at Syracuse University. She has taught introductory journalism as an adjunct instructor at Newhouse.*

Sometimes It Pays
to Hold Back

Wallace D. Beene

Never try to get ahead of the police. Despite all the movies and TV shows about journalists dashing about and solving crimes, you should remember to let the police do their work, and then you can report what happened.

My first job was as a police reporter on the *Shreveport Times*. Soon after I started, the newsroom got a call about a man in a hotel nearby who was reportedly threatening to commit suicide. A photographer and I rushed over and found we had arrived ahead of the police. I said, "Let's go on up to the room and see what's happening."

The older, and wiser, photographer said, "No, we'll wait for the cops."

I tried again to get him to go up with me, but again he refused.

A few minutes later the cops arrived, and we went up together. They knocked on the door and a voice replied, "Come in."

The cops opened the door to see a man bend over the foot of the bed. Across the foot of the bed was taped a shotgun.

The man put his head in front of the barrel and jerked a cloth tape tied to the trigger. The tape broke, and the two officers lunged forward to stop him from reaching the trigger with his hand. They risked their lives falling on top of him in front of the gun, while I stood there in shock.

To this day I can visualize standing there while the guy blew his brains all over the wall. That's why I tell my students, "Never try to get ahead of the cops.

Wallace D. Beene retired in 1993 from the journalism faculty at the University of Arizona in Tucson. He was a reporter at the Shreveport Times, Shreveport Journal, New Orleans Item, *and* Tucson Citizen. *He was a correspondent in Europe for six years and in Vietnam for two years.*

Don't Write a Check
with Your Mouth
that Your Actions Can't Cash

David H. Nimmer

We'd been talking in my broadcast reporting class that morning about sources: how to find them, how to get information from them and how to keep them, without sacrificing the reporter's integrity.

The truth is, in this session, I'd been doing all the talking and the students had been listening—sort of, with their chins in their hands and their eyes on the wall.

My lecture was straight out of Melvin Mencher's textbook, *News Reporting and Writing,* from Chapter 12 on "Finding, Cultivating and Using Sources."

His book is insightful and the lecture was thoughtful, but the students looked bored as hell.

"The sources," I intoned, "are the reporter's lifeblood. You ought not to get too close to 'em, but you are obligated to keep from hanging 'em out to dry."

I stopped to collect my thoughts: I was preaching again, and the congregation was damned near asleep. I took a piece of paper from my lecture notes and folded it.

"I have here in my hand a copy of the criminal record of a candidate for lieutenant governor. Who wants it?" I asked. Fifteen pairs of hands reached out.

"Not so fast," I said. "If you take this, you don't know where you got it."

"What do you mean?" said one of the students with his hand out the farthest.

"I mean that I don't want you using my name. I want you to keep my confidentiality. I don't want you telling anyone where you got this," I replied.

43

A single student pulled back her hand. Fourteen others were willing to make the bargain. So I told them about Dan Cohen, one of the best sources I ever had and a source who got burned badly enough to take his grievance all the way to the U.S. Supreme Court—and win. But the story began eight years earlier.

It was a gray, cold morning on October 27, 1982, and I was sitting at my desk in the basement studios at WCCO Television, about to head over to the "cop shop" and make my reporter rounds. The phone rang.

"Dave, it's Cohen. Can you meet me for lunch downtown? I've got a document relating to the governor's campaign that you ought to see." I told him I was on my way.

We met at the counter of a bank cafeteria. Cohen handed me the document and muttered the usual "you-don't-know-where-you-got-this" admonition. I nodded. Cohen and I had been through this mating dance before, since 1965, when he was a member of the city council. Over the years, Cohen slipped me a number of documents: planning reports, consultants' studies and preformance reviews. He was a rebel, a maverick who seemed to relish exposing the underbelly of city government.

On this day in October, he was peddling something I didn't want. The document he gave me turned out to be a criminal complaint against Marlene Johnson, the Democratic-Farmer-Labor candidate for lieutenant governor. It was a conviction for shoplifting six dollars' worth of sewing supplies twelve years earlier.

I knew that Cohen was working on the campaign of Wheelock Whitney, the Independent-Republican candidate running for governor against Rudy Perpich and his running mate Marlene Johnson.

"This isn't exactly a smoking gun," I told Cohen. "But I'll take it back to the station and see what the assignment editor thinks." Cohen told me to do whatever I wanted and said he had given the record to three other reporters—from the AP, the *Minneapolis Star Tribune* and the *St. Paul Pioneer Press*. I think I picked up the check and we parted. I didn't run back to the station, I walked. This was no story. This charge was too old. And the crime was too petty. We'd throw this in the wastebasket.

When I got back, the news director, the assignment editor and the executive producer all agreed: this story wouldn't see the airwaves. And we couldn't imagine any of the other media would bite.

But what we didn't know was there were other discussions going on in the newsrooms of the *Pioneer Press* and the *Star Tribune*. There, editors were deciding that Cohen, and his attempts to peddle this smear sheet, were a part of the story and, in fact, made it newsworthy.

About five o'clock that afternoon, Cohen called me at the station. "The papers are going to use my name," he said. "They're going to screw me over." He asked me whether we were going to use the story. I said, no.

The next day, over their reporters' objections, the *Star Tribune* and *Pioneer Press* published stories about Johnson's misdemeanor record, naming Cohen as the source of the information. The Associated Press also published the story but did not use Cohen's name.

And later that day, Dan Cohen resigned from his job as public relations director for Martin-Williams Advertising, Inc.

I remember being angry, because the papers published the story and because they identified Cohen, breaking the promise their reporters made. I called an editor friend of mine at the *Pioneer Press*.

"What the hell are you doing?" I complained. "I know you don't like Dan Cohen, but that's no reason to hang him out to dry like this." She told me to calm down and explained the reasoning.

The real story, she said, was the fact that an operative of the Whitney campaign (Cohen) was running around in a last ditch effort to discredit the DFL gubernatorial ticket. She said that the promise of confidentiality was ill-advised because Cohen had given the information to four reporters.

"He spread the stuff all over town," she said. "How can something like that be confidential?" I replied that a promise is a promise, and when her reporter promised, he knew that others were going to get the same criminal complaint.

We agreed to disagree so we didn't have the argument over whether the reporters should have checked with their editors before making the promise of confidentiality. My editor friend and I had been reporters for too long to believe that the veterans, at least, needed to get permission.

And the papers' reporters were veterans, angry over their editors' decisions to name Cohen. Such a move, they would later argue, hurt their credibility with sources and diminished their roles as professionals.

Cohen was aware of the dispute within the newsrooms when he filed a lawsuit against the parent companies of the two papers on December 15, 1982, claiming fraud and breach of contract for naming him as a source of the Johnson story.

It took five-and-a-half years for the case to go to trial. It took less than a month before I felt its implications on my police beat. I was in the homicide division, in the generally unfriendly confines behind a piece of Plexiglass and the vacant stares of a secretary at the front desk. I was seeking information about the continuing investigation of a particularly brutal murder of an elderly couple in south Minneapolis.

One of the detectives I'd known for several years took out the case file and began telling me about the police canvass of the neighborhood, looking for witnesses.

"You'd better be careful with him," said a young, grim-faced lieutenant, in a voice loud enough for everyone in the room to hear. "You can't trust these reporters. Just ask Dan Cohen."

The detective continued looking through the file and talking. I got the tidbit of information I was seeking, thanked the detective and stopped by the lieutenant's desk on my way out. "Just for your information," I snapped, "I've been keeping promises to sources for more than twenty years." Damn, I was angry.

And I was still harboring a few resentments over the fallout from the Cohen case when I was called to the witness stand in July, 1988, midway through the trial.

Responding to questions from Cohen's attorney, I told the jury that Cohen had made a specific request for confidentiality in the Marlene Johnson matter and that I understood we had a bargain, a verbal contract.

I also said I believed the newspapers' editors never thought much of Cohen because he'd been critical of the local press in the past—in a particularly galling and smart-aleck manner.

I got off the stand without a single question from the lead lawyer for the newspapers, a well-dressed, smooth-talking partner from one of the Twin Cities prestigious law firms. Cohen's lawyer, on the other hand, was a former defeated candidate for attorney general, dressed in a rumpled sport coat and storing his documents and papers in a shopping bag under the desk in the courtroom.

As I walked out, I took a last look at the jury and I had a hunch that proved correct: On July 22, the six members ruled in Cohen's favor, awarding him $200,000 for the loss of his job and a half million dollars in punitive damages (punishment for failing to protect his identity).

For the next three years, the case bounced around on appeal—from the state Court of Appeals to the Minnesota Supreme Court to the U.S. Supreme Court. On June 24, 1991, the country's highest court ruled five to four that reporters' promises of confidentiality are legally binding despite First Amendment protections. And on January 23, 1991, almost ten years after his lawsuit was filed, Cohen was awarded $200,000 in damages by the Minnesota Supreme Court.

When the final order came down, I was in the middle of my second year of teaching journalism at St. Thomas. And now, my war story had an ending—in fact, it had a pretty big finish.

The consequences were not lost on my class of young, would-be reporters, a half-dozen of whom, by now, were leaning forward in their chairs with their hands waving in the air.

"So," said one, "what would you have done if your news director ordered you to write about Cohen, as the source of the criminal record?"

I hesitated. "I'd like to think," I said to the class, "that I would have threatened to quit if my boss ordered me to name my source." That sounded like grandstanding to another student.

"Why didn't you just check with your news director in advance," she said, "before you made the deal with Cohen? Then you wouldn't have the dilemma." Well, that question pushed one of my reporter's buttons. "Because," I said, "I'd been on the street asking questions when he was in grade school. That's why." Even I had to admit that sounded a little angry—after several students noticed and said something.

Our discussion was getting lively and thoughtful. One of the seniors in the class pointed out there was a compromise between the reporter protecting the source (Cohen) and the boss wanting to reveal his political dirty trick.

"You could've written the story saying the information came from a member of her (Marlene Johnson) opponent's campaign team," he said. "That says something about the ulterior motive without naming Cohen."

In the next half hour, the students and I walked an ethical bramble patch that I'd encountered, but never thought much about while I was practicing the reporter's craft. We talked of the editors' obligations—or whether there were any—to honor their reporters' promises. We discussed what to do when reporters made bad judgments, as the majority of the class thought I had when I so easily promised Cohen confidentiality.

We also talked about the nature of reporter autonomy, one of the questions posed in a case study by Stanford Professor Ted Glasser in the book *Media Ethics* (issues and cases). As a former reporter, I wanted to make a decision to protect a source on the street, by myself, and right now; the students were more willing to wait and debate and to consult with editors and news directors before making their promises. And maybe they were wiser, at least in an increasingly litigious society.

Before the two-hour class ended, we did reach some conclusions:

- that reporters and newsroom managers ought to be talking more—in advance—about how to deal with ethical issues;

- that the whole process of granting anonymity ought to be conducted in a more thoughtful manner;

- that reporters must face the truth that in the Nineties, editors and producers are taking more and more authority over the news product and how it's gathered and packaged; and finally,

- that editors and reporters all over the country now know they'd better not write a check with their mouths that their actions can't cash. Don't make the promise if you can't keep it.

As the students filed out of the classroom, I thought I couldn't have found a better way to make the point.

David Nimmer is an assistant professor of journalism at the University of St. Thomas in St. Paul, MN. He has worked as a reporter and editor at the Minneapolis Star *and as a reporter, associate news director, and talk show host at WCCO Television News.*

Never Can Say Goodbye

Susan Ruel

Long before anyone ever dreamed that pop star Michael Jackson might one day become Elvis Presley's son-in-law, I tried ... and tried and tried ... to become the only reporter in America to get an interview with him.

It was June 1984—the summer of the Thriller tour—and I had just been promoted to the foreign desk of United Press International in Washington, D.C. It occurred to me that by phoning the "Godfather of Soul," James Brown, whom I had once interviewed in San Francisco, I might be able to use Brown as a go-between to get to Jackson, the Man of the Hour, who had just set the all-time world record for most albums sold.

Mr. Brown was cordial. He advised me that my best bet would be to contact a guy I'd never heard of, someone by the name of the Reverend Al Sharpton.

It took me more than a few tries to get through to Sharpton's New York office. They gave me a number where I could reach the reverend. He was staying with the Jackson entourage in a Texas hotel. So far, so good. I got in touch with him in Dallas, invoked the name of James Brown, and was assured that it just might be possible to schedule an exclusive with the elusive Michael Jackson.

"Call me back Sunday afternoon at about three o'clock, and I'll let you know Michael's decision," he said.

Sunday afternoon found me at a picnic, where I kept excusing myself to use the host's telephone. Billing all charges to my home number, I tried to get through to the Reverend Al. Beginning at 3 P.M., I phoned every half-hour. Late that evening, I got Sharpton's wife, who told me to try back the next morning. I did, and they had checked out.

49

Not one to be daunted easily, I traced the Thriller tour to St. Louis. I called every major hotel until I tracked down the Jackson party—and Sharpton.

"I'm gonna talk to Michael in the limo tonight after the show," he said, promisingly. "Be sure to call me tomorrow afternoon, and I'll give you the time and place for the interview."

Several days and several cities later, I tracked him down again. He *was* hard to reach, but hey, anyone important enough to go on tour with the Gloved One had to be sought after, I told myself—and my somewhat skeptical editor. UPI was on the skids financially, so I signed up for an el-cheapo flight out of Baltimore that would get me into Kansas City in time for an afternoon interview the following Tuesday, as Sharpton had arranged.

I was working the deep overnight shift that summer, but spent my free time poring over clippings about Billie Jean's love object, and the lyrics to all of Michael's hits. Feeling a trifle frivolous, I set aside stories on Chinese dissidents and the hostages in Lebanon to trace the history of the Jackson Five. Finally, I honed my list of questions down to twenty and put them in the proper ascending order of offensiveness. My brush with history was approaching.

After a few futile attempts to confirm my rendezvous with destiny, I decided to cross-check the interview with one Frank DeLeo, whom the newspapers described as perhaps even closer to Michael than Sharpton himself. The hotel switchboard put me through to DeLeo's room. Miraculously, he answered on the first ring.

"Hello, this is Susan Ruel of UPI. Just calling to say how thrill—I mean *grateful*—we are that Michael has agreed to let us do the interview. I want to confirm it for 2 P.M. Tuesday in Kansas City."

"I don't know who made that kind of promise, but I can assure you that Mr. Jackson absolutely will grant no interviews," DeLeo said. At least he said it nicely.

It was the season of UPI's first declaration of bankruptcy. My paychecks hadn't started bouncing yet, but money was very tight. UPI's chagrin at missing a chance to uphold the reputation of their once hallowed wire service by scooping The Associated Press mingled with relief at being able to save the price of a plane ticket from Baltimore to Kansas City.

Sometimes you have to know when to quit. Quit trying to get an interview with Michael Jackson, that is, not quit UPI.

Susan Ruel, Ph.D., is an assistant professor of English/journalism at the University of Delaware. She has worked for UPI and the AP in Shanghai, San Francisco, Washington, and New York.

Persistence

All of these stories show how persistence pays off. If you haven't got persistence, you probably won't get a job in journalism in the first place. It's the people who really keep at it who get the jobs—and the good stories.

Bill Gruver fought obstacles for six months to get an interview with former President Ronald Reagan. And he refused to take other people's word for it that the meeting would be a waste of time. He got his interview, and it proved to be far better than he had expected.

Laurie O'Brien doggedly developed her photography skills until she was assigned to cover the presidential primary in New Hampshire. She then persisted through months of following candidates day and night, becoming a competent and respected photographer for her efforts.

If Ron Pruitt hadn't continued to question and dig deeper into what seemed to be a routine story, he never would have discovered that the story was much more than it had initially appeared. It's always a good idea to proceed as if there could be more behind every story. If some unanswered question keeps sticking in your mind—*Why* did he do it?—poke around until you find out.

Robin Andersen discovered that digging deeper often means breaking away from the pack. By doing its own leg work and not waiting for "official" sources to hand-feed it information, a freelance news team in Nicaragua was able to get what no one else did—a great shot of Fidel Castro. Too often reporters tend to hang together because it is safer, easier, and more fun. But that is also a way to become lazy. If you think there's a good story out there, don't wait for it to come to you. Go out and find it.

Or, as Pete Benjaminson did, keep calling until you get it. He certainly didn't let a little thing like being hung up on twice stop him from getting his information.

Going One-On-One with Reagan

Bill Gruver

I had been warned that an interview with Ronald Reagan would be a waste of time because the former president wouldn't remember anything and would fall asleep before our talk was over. But I needed to talk to him for a book I was writing about the most controversial member of his administration, Ed Meese, the White House counselor and later attorney general. For six months I fought the obstacles thrown at me by his aides before I finally got to judge Reagan for myself.

Contrary to what I had been told, I found him to be a man without guise. He was personable and affable, but that didn't mean he wasn't serious. He was a good reader and a good observer of other people. He did not strike a pose, as do so many political people, when being interviewed. He had no fear or suspicion of microphones or cameras. He didn't, in person, have an adversarial feeling when being asked about his views or what he did. That made interviewing Reagan easier. He was not complex, but contrary to what many pundits claim, he did have a grasp of major events. It's just that he believed his staff should do the plodding research work and that he needn't be involved.

I had been told by many colleagues that Reagan wouldn't remember facts or dates and would be fuzzy about details. He was described as a charming man without intellect whose smile and movie star status was the key to his success. And I was told the interview would be short and Reagan would stretch his answers with long-winded stories, forgetting the questions.

First of all, Reagan didn't listen to his aides about time limitations. "I'll call you when we have finished," was the way he told them to leave us alone, which didn't make those aides very happy. They must have thought some deep, dark secrets would be given away. He told me I could ask any question about anything, and he never said, "No comment." He answered every question directly. He even quoted my memo to him of some months earlier. He recalled, in vivid detail, every event we discussed; he had no notes. He didn't try to rush me, but kept a conversational tone and mood throughout the interview. He also avoided giving bad reviews to any who served him.

It took nearly six months to arrange and confirm my interview with Reagan because his staff wanted to have my questions in advance. I refused to give them because it would have been unethical and compromising. I did agree to list the topics of my interest, but they backed off. Reagan had no concern about my questions or topics. At the outset of the interview he said to me, "Why did it take so long for us to meet?"

Reagan was proud of the fact that as the nation's number one Republican he could praise FDR and JFK and get away with it. His own credentials as a once-loyal Democrat who left that party because it moved too far to the left for his taste was for him a badge of honor, and it is what probably attracted millions of Americans who felt the same way. Reagan regarded himself, although a distinctly conservative Republican, as a man who could bridge party differences, and spoke about that proudly.

When we talked about Ed Meese, Reagan was generous. He said he could trust Meese because they were on the same wavelength. He said he never considered those who urged him to fire Meese. He wanted, he said, Meese's "valuable advice. I could count on him to cut through layers of reports and provide a bottom line."

He was bitter about the media attacks made on his secretary of labor, Ray Donovan, before his indictment and after his acquittal. "Too often you are guilty first according to media reports," Reagan said.

But the most impressive thing about this one-on-one with Reagan was to see how he looked. He looked like sixty-five instead of a man in his mid-eighties. He had the handshake of a gorilla and the figure of a much younger man. I got the impression that the key to Reagan's successful personality was that he didn't take himself too seriously. He maintained his informal demeanor and made his guest feel at ease. I was advised by many of my colleagues that waiting and trying so hard to get the Reagan interview wasn't worth the effort. However, I felt that Reagan's views of Meese were essential to any book about the former attorney general. Meese's loyalty to Reagan was unquestioned. It seemed to me that he would fall on his sword anytime for his leader.

It's not unusual for presidential aides to be overly protective. I have run into that situation before. But once in Reagan's presence it was all forgotten. We sat next to each other with my tape recorder between us. Unlike some other interviews I have conducted, there was no adversarial atmosphere.

I had, of course, done considerable research before the interview, covering every major book about the Reagan Presidential years. I reread the pile of clippings regarding the special relationship between Reagan and Meese.

When it finally happened, the interview with Reagan was so informal that it was more of a conversation. There was none of the confrontational atmosphere that can occur during an interview, especially with a famous person. I hadn't expected much from this interview, having had to go through so many obstacles, and Reagan certainly was not known for giving exclusive interviews. His critics claimed he couldn't maintain concentration for such an exchange.

My experience was contrary to all of the pundits' opinions. The former president was alert and, using no notes, had excellent recall of historic events. Although he didn't ask for a transcript of our discussion, I did send a summary which he said was accurate.

Reagan did show some of his reputed stubborness when it came to loyalty to those he had appointed to serve him and his administration. He never claimed he was treated badly by the press, but made it quite clear that many attacks on his aides were actually not-so-subtle attacks on him.

The waiting and the delays were worth the chance to talk to Reagan in this frank exchange. This was a glimpse into one memorable historic period.

Bill Gruver is an adjunct professor at the Walter Cronkite School of Journalism and Telecommunication at Arizona State University and a broadcast journalist representing a radio news network at the Arizona State Capital; he also writes a column which is syndicated to 110 newspapers. Previously he was a political editor at CBS News and a political editor for syndicated columnist Jack Anderson and ABC-TV's Good Morning America.

Covering Jimmy *Who?*

Laurie O'Brien

The details of the call were unimportant enough to me that I have forgotten the particulars. It was just an assignment, one that as a novice photojournalist I was eager to have. Go to Manchester, New Hampshire, said Dave Wurzel, Boston bureau chief of United Press International Newspictures, and get some shots of this guy from Georgia who was going to announce that he was running for president. Try, Wurzel emphasized, to get something interesting. No head shots, nothing posed. Something with some life in it. Sure, I said. Call you when I get back.

It was 1975. Before that year was out, there would be nine Democratic and two Republican contenders for the office Gerald Ford had assumed after the Nixon debacle. I would cover them all, racing around New Hampshire to capture on film that important common touch that American voters were beginning to expect from their politicians.

I was a twenty-six-year-old largely self-trained news photographer. I had graduated from Wellesley College four years earlier with a degree in English. I had taught school for a year in central New Hampshire, backpacked around Europe for a few months, and worked for a couple of years as a photographer for a New Hampshire ski resort that was owned by the nephew of Tommy the Cork, one of Franklin Roosevelt's henchmen. My photographic training had begun in the laboratory of a physician department head at the University of Tennessee Medical School during a summer job when I was in college. When I wasn't helping my boss cut up cats and study the results of the operations on computer printouts, I was taking and developing lecture slides for his physiology and biophysics classes. The photographic content wasn't terribly exciting, but the job got me started as a competent darkroom techician. Then I had an apprenticeship with a photographer on Cape Cod who combined aerial work and society weddings. I learned how to make really big prints (*very* carefully) and distinguish virtually identical brides. Once again, I learned more craft than content. Only when I went to work at Waterville Valley Ski Area did I have the chance to work with candid, moving subjects. I was hooked.

Of course, there were the obligatory public relations shots—the turkey going up the chairlift just before Thanksgiving, people on roller skis during a snow drought, the Easter Bunny on skis—but I also shot a lot of action. Waterville Valley was a World Cup site, and competitive freestyle skiing was born there. The resort sent out photos as press releases every week during the ski season and used a clipping service to track the results. Before long, I was seeing my photos running in newspapers all over the country and occasionally abroad. I became an expert on stuffing photographic gear in my pockets and toting it on my back. I got thoroughly used to adverse weather conditions (film freezes before feet do). I got good at finding photo possibilities where none exist. And I fell in love with capturing on film what I could see in my mind and through my viewfinder.

After a lot of sports and a few chances at news (mountain rescues, fires, that sort of thing), I headed down from the White Mountains of New Hampshire to the UPI bureau in Boston. I wanted a job. Wurzel, a large, graying man with an abrupt demeanor, took me on. It wasn't a real job, of course. UPI only had about fifty photographers in the whole country. Nobody, it appeared, ever quit or even had the decency to die. I would have to start as a stringer and work my way up. That was fine with me. Wurzel loaded my arms with orange Kodak boxes of film and paper and toted the fifty-five-pound portable Photofax machine down to my car. I was in business.

Business was predictably slow. Nothing happens in New Hampshire. The covered bridges get older, the occasional farmer has the photographic sense to mow his fields with beautiful teams of Belgian horses, and on a slow day you can turn up the odd chain saw sculpturer and get a shot that will make the wire. But nothing really happens. Except every four years when New Hampshire hosts the first-in-the-nation presidential primary.

Wurzel was a little early. I started in the spring, and heavy primary activity wasn't expected until the following winter, but I suppose he figured he couldn't always turn up a photographic newshound on short notice. I guess he decided he'd rather be ready early.

Let me say now that I didn't know much about the news business. I kept up, I read the newspaper, but I wasn't formally trained in newsgathering. I blithely assumed everybody else knew what they were doing. And since I considered myself a quick study, I thought I'd figure it out.

Jimmy Carter in the summer of 1975 was hardly a household name. A small press contingent gathered for his news conference in Manchester. Accompanied by Jody Powell, who was to be his driver, advance man, press aide, and coffee-carrier for the next few months, Carter announced his intentions. The TV guys got their sound bites, the reporters scribbled in their little notebooks, and all I got was a couple of head shots. Not at all what Wurzel wanted. Surely, I thought, something will happen, someone will at least suggest something. Surely this man who wants to be president knows enough to *do* something.

But no. There was some polite milling around, but no action. I didn't know Dave Wurzel very well, but I knew him well enough to know this wasn't what he had in mind. I stepped up to Jody Powell. "Do you think Mr. Carter might do some campaigning?"

What did I have in mind?

"Get out from behind the podium, leave the building, walk around the block, shake hands." Surely, I thought, a picture possibility will open up. I can't go back with just head shots. Wurzel will kill me. No, Wurzel will fire me. And I haven't even gotten started yet.

Off we went around the small city block in downtown Manchester. The older news pros were bored. They had what they needed but were reluctant to leave in case anything happened. Jody Powell was eager and accommodating. "In here? How about this diner?" Carter was grinning (always) and nervous. He cruised the counter and slipped into a booth in a coffee shop. "Hi. My name's Jimmy Carter, and I'm running for president." Experienced locals, they caught the last part, but not the first. Jimmy *Who?*

During the next months I was to accompany Carter and the other aspirants (our favorite cutline description that year) all over New Hampshire. I rode in the back seat of a rental car with Jimmy and Jody to Peterborough on the New Hampshire seacoast to meet the folks who had planted a field of peanuts and wanted the former governor of Georgia to come for the harvest. He did, and bent down in his navy blue suit over the bushy furrows to hoist up a dirty handful of peanut plants, a trophy of sorts for both him and me. I followed Carter through tack, nail, gun, and match factories, catching him donning various protective gear, learning to angle around machines to get my shots. I hovered as he campaigned in old folks' homes, schools, churches, and even a formal wear shop. I sent out photos of him shaking hands with a meter maid who was ticketing his car (Jody paid the ticket) and handing campaign brochures to a tuxedo-clad store window dummy. Late one night I photographed Carter when he stayed in the home of supporters in Concord. It was late in the primary season, and the campaign days were long. His feet were propped on a desk, and a hole showed clearly in the sole of his shoe. "Just like Adlai Stevenson," Wurzel said, as the shot emerged on the wire in the Boston bureau. I was doing okay.

The tenor of the campaign changed during the fall and winter. What started out as a cozy threesome grew to multibus proportions by February and the approaching primary day. There were eleven major campaigners, including the sitting president who was having to work hard this time around. Having learned early, thanks to Jimmy and Jody and their easy approachability, to ask for what I wanted in the way of shots, I grew more confident. I called various campaign headquarters, learned who would be in the state each day, and plotted the best itineraries. I learned the photographic hazards of the best New Hampshire political attractions. Textile factories were full of dust and lint and could produce negatives that were difficult to print if you weren't careful. Press buses were packed with TV types who could run down photographers and print reporters with ease. Secret service men didn't like jokes about pistol grips on motorized Nikons. And no matter how exciting, tedious, stimulating or wearing any day of a presidential campaign was, for the photographers it always ended in a final rush—developing film in a strange hotel bathroom, printing wet negatives, and dictating cutlines while a colleague called New York to explain what we were getting ready to transmit.

I learned a lot of things on the campaign trail with Jimmy Carter. I learned to pay attention and not assume that people who'd been covering the news necessarily knew more than a newcomer with fresh perspective and a strong desire to please a picky boss. An urgent phone message relayed to me when the press bus stopped often meant a request for a certain kind of shot. Sometimes this meant Wurzel had simply thought of something that might prove possible and interesting. Sometimes it was a result of his perusal of other major dailies; a photographic idea displayed on page one of the *Boston Globe* would inspire him to suggest a spin-off. Sometimes his requests were a response to pictures coming in on the wire from other parts of the campaign. When President Ford went skiing in Aspen, he called urgently for snow pictures of Ronald Reagan campaigning in New Hampshire. "Reagan wouldn't get on skis? Then how about getting him to throw a snowball?" I was less intimidated by campaign managers than I was by the seasoned UPI photographers on the other end of the phone. I waited, begged, and cajoled for my snow pictures, and by the time the New Hampshire voters went to the polls, I had a full set, every candidate running and his encounters with New Hampshire weather.

Was this news? Not in the sense that world opinion changes when people see candidate Carter trudging through a blizzard or tossing a handful of white stuff. And yet, in a curious way, it was important. It was a chance for me to see, up very close and over a long period of time, how a man who wants to be president reacts to people and the world around him. Carter with his peanuts and his snow was silly, just like we were when we asked for the "photo ops" that kept our editors satisfied. But over grueling months of campaigning, from those early days of Jimmy *Who?* when nobody knew who he was to the final week when he was just beginning to be taken seriously, he maintained a warm demeanor at a high energy pace.

Print reporters on the campaign trail toiled over drafts of speeches, distilling the political ideology, combing the text for questions and incongruities. TV reporters, umbilically tied together in those days by sound cords and wielding large cameras, strove for the minute-and-a-half flashes that would bring the sharpest focus of the campaign day into America's living rooms. The still photographers traveled light—jackets with a lot of pockets, small backpacks, and maybe one additional bag that stayed on the bus and contained mostly backup gear. They could run at a quick clip with their arms steadying the three or four Nikons that hung around their necks. They were eager, alert, professional, and not terribly talkative. The soft whir of their motor drives was an unvarying predictor of something happening. I loved them. I wanted to scoop every one of them, every day, at every campaign stop. But I still loved them. They taught me to run fast, shoot steadily, and wait patiently when I had to. They also taught me to respect a profession that allowed me such a close look at the governing process. And they taught me to respect the people in high office but never feel subservient. They taught me to get my shots.

I was at the airport the morning after Carter's impressive win in New Hampshire. "How about a victory sign, Governor?" Carter flashed the two-fingered V and grinned as he headed for the plane. My shot ran a few days later in both *Time* and *Newsweek*. I began to think I knew a little something about news after all.

After the 1975 presidential primary ended, I continued to work for UPI out of the Boston bureau. I did a lot of candid feature work and went down to Boston for some of the bicentennial events. I covered the first tall ships entering Boston Harbor, Queen Elizabeth's visit, and a few other news events. But life was slowing down, and after the excitement of the campaign, I had trouble with covered bridges and hay fields. So I headed for Atlanta with the promise of work through a New York photo agency that specialized in news.

It was good to be back in the fast lane. Carter was gone a lot, but when he was in Georgia, there were baseball games every Sunday in Plains and plenty of encounters with his eager-to-be-photographed family. I shot Billy and his gas station, Miss Lillian, Rosalynn, Amy, and the rest of the gang. I covered the election night festivities when Carter came out victorious over Ford. But none of it was ever as much fun as New Hampshire. Politics was big business. I missed the intimacy of the Portsmouth peanut harvest. I realized, though, that I had had the privilege of seeing a campaign take shape. Like most good photographers, I had been lucky to be in the right place at the right time.

Laurie O'Brien directs the Creative and Professional Writing Program at the University of West Florida where she teaches literature and writing. She worked as a news photographer for UPI, the Concord (NH) Monitor, *and Camera 5 Photo Agency. Her poetry has appeared in* Poetry, Southern Review, Mississippi Review, *and other magazines. Her first collection of poetry is* Rogues' Codes.

On Digging Deeper

Ron Pruitt

One afternoon of a slow news day I was lazing around the newsroom at the *Muskogee Daily Phoenix,* not really doing much. Noticing my inactivity the city editor approached me with a lead. He said there had been a suicide in a nearby town and asked if I would check it out. He gave me the obit information.

I had done suicide stories before and they were fairly routine. Usually they were only a few column inches in length and were always buried on the back pages of the paper. No big deal.

I first tried to call the home of the deceased man and got no answer. So I called the funeral home handling the arrangements and began asking the usual when, where, who, why, and how questions.

The funeral director told me the man had backed his car up to the laundry room of his home and hooked up a vacuum cleaner hose to the tailpile. He ran the hose through a window, left the engine running, and went into the laundry room and shut the door. His wife found him there a few hours later, dead of carbon monoxide poisoning.

The man had lived in Wagoner, Oklahoma, and commuted to his job in Tulsa where he worked at the American Airlines maintenance facility. When I asked the funeral director if anyone knew why the man had killed himself he gave me a startling reply.

He told me the man had felt guilty because he had done some work on an American Airlines passenger jet, and that the plane had subsequently crashed. He felt somehow that the crash was his fault.

That piqued my interest and I decided to pursue the story, to try to make it more than just another suicide story. I found out the wife had scheduled an appointment at the funeral home later that day. When the appointed time arrived I called back, and the wife talked to me about her husband's death.

61

She confirmed what the funeral director had told me. Her husband had been the crew chief in charge of installing an engine on a large commercial passenger plane. He felt responsible for the air crash a few days later which had killed more than 350 people. At the time it was the largest loss of life in any air crash on American soil. After asking all the questions I could think of, I asked if I could call back the next day, realizing I had an interesting story which would probably require a follow-up. She agreed to a second interview in person instead of on the phone.

I vividly remembered the crash because it had been a major national story not very long before. I went to the morgue file and began digging out stories. I found out that there had been a controversy over the crash because investigators questioned the manner in which the engine had been installed. The crew which attached the engine to the wing used improper procedures which caused the engine pylon—the structure which holds the engine onto the wing—to crack. When the plane tried to take off in Chicago a few days later, the engine fell off, and the plane went down.

I told my city editor what I had found out and he told me to keep working on the story until deadline. I attempted to call American Airlines company officials, but they stonewalled, refusing to talk. I was able to talk to some coworkers, including one member of the crew that installed the engine. He provided additional confirmation of the information I had.

I turned in the story about 10 P.M. and, after my city editor had read it, headed home for the day. The drive home was about thirty miles, and I used it, as I usually did, to unwind from a frantic day of newspaper work and think about what had happened.

When I got home, I walked into the house and flipped on the television, ready to relax. The late news out of WGN-TV, Chicago, was coming on. Guess what their lead story was.

You guessed it. In the forty-five minutes it had taken me to drive home, my story had been grabbed by the national wire and now it was big news in Chicago, where the crash had happened. I sat back and heard my own words being repeated over the tube. I have to say it was exhilarating to think millions of people in Chicago and around the country were being touched by my story.

My experience with this story illustrates two things I now tell my students. First, and most important, a story that at first appears to be no more than mundane can sometimes take on new dimensions when it is put in context with new information. This suicide story could easily have been lost in the shuffle if it had been given short shrift.

Second, always get as much information as you can in the initial interview. After the media attention generated by the first day's story, the wife reneged on her promise to allow another interview. I never talked to her again.

Ron Pruitt has taught journalism at Pittsburg State University in Kansas. He worked for the Muskogee Daily Phoenix *and as radio news director at KTLQ-AM and KEOK-FM in eastern Oklahoma.*

Doing the Legwork in Nicaragua

Robin K. Andersen

Tension cut through the hot, humid air, filling the morning with anticipation. In a flurry of activity, reporters scurried through the hotel lobby, formed small groups, broke apart, and formed others. Everybody wanted to find the right companions for the day's search. Nicaragua was celebrating the first anniversary of the overthrow of the dictator, Anastasio Somoza, and the foreign press had converged on the capital. The El Camino Real, one of Managua's few international hotels, was swarming with reporters, camera crews, still photographers and freelance journalists. It was a few days after the main celebration of July 19, which had attracted many international dignitaries. The press, cordoned off in an area ripe for photo-opportunities, had attended the day-long festivities of political speeches, and the parade filled with neighborhood floats, high school bands, wounded veterans of the insurrection, and dancers who had come all the way from the Atlantic coast. There had also been a show of military hardware, tanks, and personnel carriers, creating for the cameras just the images needed to encourage the warning beginning to emanate from Washington that the Sandinista revolutionaries had the "domination of the hemisphere" in mind. (History would show, however, that such assertions were far more the construct of the U.S. government than they ever were the intention of the Sandinista government.)

Finding pictures as good as those was not going to be easy. What every journalist was hoping for was to find the elusive Fidel Castro. To catch up with him, camera in hand, would be the real prize. Talking to him would be an added bonus—a sound bite or two would have been nice. But it would be translated or voiced over anyway. In addition, having made one of the longest speeches the day of the celebration, Castro had already confirmed his support for and solidarity with his Nicaraguan counterparts. So the hope

64

was for a picture, one closer than the press pit had allowed, of Castro the Communist, mingling with the Nicaraguans.

Castro was news by virtue of his fit over the agenda being set in Washington. As one TV anchorperson explained, there was only so much airtime for television news, and Nicaragua was competing with news from all other foreign countries for the five-to-seven minutes allotted international coverage. There would be very limited tolerance on the part of editors for background stories on the country and its people. It was 1980, and Central America was poised to become an "important geographical region" and the focus of U.S. foreign policy.

Already days had passed since the celebration, and no one had seen Fidel Castro. To make matters worse, the Sandinista press liaisons were not offering his itinerary, and there was no press conference scheduled. It was the beginning of what would become very bad press relations with the new government (which went a long way to explain the negative press coverage of the years of Sandinista rule). The only thing that had leaked was an official meeting he was to attend later in the week. But most journalists were not planning to stay that long. Every day had begun with anticipation, as journalists set off with great determination in a variety of different rented vehicles. But each day ended with disappointment. Wild rumors had begun to spread, some speculating that he was not in Nicaragua at all, but flying back and forth to Cuba, possibly on a daily basis.

Breakfast at the El Camino was abuzz with calculation as journalists speculated where they might find him. Local celebrations were taking place in the small towns around Managua, and some thought he might attend one of them. Nobody really knew, but many members of the press corps looked to the network crews. After all, they had the money to rent the best vehicles and hire local "stringers." They could also pay for tips— from government officials to Nicaraguan campesinos.

A variety of freelancers were trying to hop rides with network vehicles. Other journalists watched the morning activities with a careful eye, hoping to follow anyone who looked like they had a clue. Some decided not to try at all, choosing instead to wait for some official word.

I watched these strange routines of the foreign press corps with estranged fascination. My composure, in the face of the morning's pressure, stemmed from my detachment. I wasn't worried about the story. For me, *they* were the story. I was a graduate student doing field work for my Ph.D. dissertation. As I "spied" on them, attempting to discern the rules of this particular set of "newsgathering" practices, it became clear that, in lieu of official information, looking to the network crews was standard procedure—the thing to do. But the network crews had begun to lose interest. They made a short run in the afternoon around town, then came back to the hotel, hoping to find some "official" information about Castro. Some other journalists also decided to stay behind.

I went out that day with a couple of freelancers, searching the surrounding small towns for the Cuban leader. By afternoon we decided to stay put in a little community where Nicaraguans waited patiently behind banners that welcomed Castro. Everyone there expected him to come. As the hours wore on, I learned a great deal about the country and its people. They were eager to explain why deposing such a brutal dictator was good for them. They wanted not so much friends, but help and recognition of their determination to be an independent country. One of the most striking images of the day was the way the police sat and waited with the children of the community. Together, everyone talked, laughed, played, and never did see Fidel Castro. By the time we returned to the hotel, well after dark, we heard the triumphant story of the journalists who found him. A group of freelancers was driving in the countryside, saw the official caravan, and followed it. By running across a field to thwart security guards, they arrived in front of a large finca where Castro had been invited to lunch. The journalists were invited to stay, and one of the photographers snapped a shot of Castro eating a piece of meat off the end of a knife. She sold the picture to one of the large international photo agencies.

My study of newsgathering practices, in Nicaragua and elsewhere, taught me that the willingness to do the legwork needed to gather the news is one of the most important attributes of a good journalist. It separates good reporters from those who come to rely too heavily on official information. Those who look to the networks and their sources can miss the real story just as easily. Many times foreign reporters never leave their hotels for fear of missing the latest leak or release. Too often material from official sources is not verified.

In Nicaragua, those who chose to stay at the hotel and wait got no story at all. But those who did find Castro, in a sense, also missed the story. During the afternoon I spent in that small Nicaraguan town, I learned more from the people about who they were, what they wanted and how they felt about politics and their country than I ever would have from all the "official" documents and dignitaries. All too often the agenda for coverage of foreign countries is set in Washington.

Robin Andersen, Ph.D., is chairwoman of the communications department at Fordham University. Her book, Consumer Culture and Television Programming, *was published by Westview Press in 1995, and her articles have appeared in books and scholarly journals such as* The Media Reader, Journalism and Popular Culture, Media Culture and Society, Latin American Perspectives, Social Text, EXTRA!, *and the* Humanist.

Criss-cross

Peter Benjaminson

When teaching my investigative reporting class, I try to introduce as many public records as possible, because they're what students are most unfamiliar with. I present them as ways of finding out what's going on under the surface of society, i.e., under the place where the PR people dwell. Some of these records, though, have uses other than the investigative.

For instance, as night editor for the *Atlanta Journal*, I had only one reporter at my disposal. But Atlanta's a big, active place and, occasionally, more than one event would occur at one time, even on my Sunday evening editing shift. Sometimes one of these events would be a fire, maybe even two, and maybe even on the opposite sides of town. With one reporter, one editor, and a rigid deadline, covering two things at once was a problem. I'd want a reporter at the scene of an important fire, but I didn't want him or her missing another event to cover a grass fire or a smoking oven. You could listen to the Fire Department's broadcasts, of course, but they were often uninformative or unintelligible. Was it a vacant building burning, or an orphanage?

The best way to find out, on short notice and without sending a reporter to non-hell and back, was the criss-cross or city directory. Produced, I'm sure, mainly for door-to-door salespeople, the criss-cross listed addresses in alphabetical and then numerical order. If you wanted to look up 10 Jones Street, you'd go to "J" for Jones, then look for "10". After the "10" you'd see the name of the person who lived there and the phone number.

With a fire and a small staff, this gave me, as night editor, two options. I could call the burning structure, after taking the address from the Fire Department broadcast. If I was lucky, someone there would answer the phone and tell me what kind of building it was. If I was really lucky, the person who answered the phone would be a movie star trapped in her bedroom with a working phone who would breathlessly feed her impressions of the fire into my tape recorder, which I always had attached to the phone waiting for just such an opportunity. (It never came.)

Usually, of course, no one would answer the phone inside the burning structure. If they were there at all, they were dead or under the bed. But the criss-cross also gave me a second chance. If I could reach the person across the street, I could ask that person to look out the window and describe the fire to me. Then I could either use his description in the story or send a reporter out there on the basis of the first-person account.

The problem was that this method often required me to call people late in the evening. The conversation would go something like this:

Ring. Ring. "Hello."

"Hello, Mrs. Smith, this is Peter Benjaminson from the *Atlanta Journal.*"

"I already have a subscription." Click.

I'd call again.

Ring. Ring. "Hello."

"DON'T HANG UP, MRS. SMITH! I'M A REPORTER. I'M NOT TRYING TO SELL YOU A SUBSCRIPTION! BUT THE FIRE DEPARTMENT TELLS ME THERE'S A *FIRE* RIGHT ACROSS THE STREET FROM *YOUR HOUSE!!* WOULD YOU PLEASE DO ME A FAVOR AND LOOK OUT YOUR WINDOW AND TELL ME WHAT YOU SEE? I'D REALLY APPRECIATE IT!"

"I'm too sleepy." Click.

I'd call again.

Ring. Ring. "Hello."

"MRS. SMITH. PLEASE. PLEASE. PLEASE. NOT ONLY WOULD IT BE THE NEIGHBORLY THING TO DO BUT THINK: THE FIRE MIGHT BE HEADING YOUR WAY. JUST GLANCE OUT THE WINDOW AND TELL ME WHAT YOU SEE!!"

Bang. Her phone drops on the floor. Bonk, bonk, bonk. (She stomps heavily to the window.) Squeak, squeak. (She pulls back the living room curtains.) AHHHHHHHHHHHHHHHHHH!? (She sees a major fire.)

I'd hang up.

"Joe," I'd say, "drop the dog show story and get out to the fire."

Another night in big-time professional journalism.

Peter Benjaminson has worked for the Redwood City Tribune, *the* Los Angeles Times, *the* Atlanta Journal, *and the* Detroit Free Press. *He was a journalism professor at the State University of New York at Binghamton, New York University, and the Graduate School of Journalism at Columbia University. He is the coauthor of* Investigative Reporting *and the author of* The Story of Motown *and* Death in the Afternoon: America's Newspaper Giants Struggle for Survival. *Benjaminson is now assistant editor of the* Chief-Leader, *New York City's civil service newspaper.*

You Never Know
Until You Try

I have often found that some of the best stories are the
most unexpected. That's why it's always dangerous to think, "Oh, he'll never
talk to me," or "I could never get that story," because you never know until
you try.

Perk Rankin found that out when he summoned up the courage to
approach one of the wealthiest and most private men in the world. He was
rewarded with a fascinating conversation with Howard Hughes.

David Dick wasn't as lucky in his attempts to get to his man, but he sure
tried. And for a while there, he got farther than any other reporter.

Like Dick, Emil Dansker used a trick to get him past hospital security. It
didn't work immediately, but in the end he got his story. And while he found
that getting into a hospital room is tough, getting into hotel rooms—twice—
can be a lot easier, if you're clever and patient.

Being willing to try, despite considerable opposition, earned Gregg
Hoffmann a national award. He believed he could make an interesting series
out of a subject his editor said was boring and would go unread. Hoffmann
didn't take his editor's word for it; he pursued the story anyway, on his own
time, and proved once again that a good reporter doesn't quit without
trying.

A Conversation with Howard Hughes

W. Parkman Rankin

It was the fall of 1951 and at the time one of my assignments as motion picture advertising manager for *This Week* magazine was to call on the movie studios in Hollywood twice a year. I was staying at the Beverly Hills Hotel and one evening around midnight, as I was strolling through the lobby, I spotted a man sitting in a side chair who I thought must be Howard Hughes, then owner of RKO Pictures. He seemed to be waiting for someone. I recall that he was tall, with a moustache, casually dressed, and good-looking.

After a while I summoned up enough courage to approach him. I introduced myself and thanked him for his current advertising business in *This Week*. He was most courteous and said it was a relief to have someone thank him for something instead of trying to sell him something. He invited me to sit down, and we started to chat. I soon discovered that he was waiting for a young lady to come out of a cocktail party. The party had been going on since 6 P.M. and it was now midnight. He would periodically send the strolling violinist in to look for the girl, but the violinist would invariably bring out the wrong one.

Hughes was slightly hard of hearing, and I had to speak clearly and distinctly. I told him I had a small presentation up in my room and asked if he would like to see it. The violinist came back with another wrong girl and Hughes said to me, "Sure, I'd like to see your presentation." I went up to my room and brought it down and went through it with him, page by page. I was soon aware that I was talking to a brilliant man. He was way ahead of me in all phases of communications and marketing.

By this time it was about 2 A.M., and I was getting sleepy. Hughes was wide awake, however, and chatted on amiably. Through all of this the

71

violinist kept bringing out young ladies, each of whom turned out to be the wrong one. Finally, I bid Hughes goodnight and went up to my room.

My only proof of this meeting is the testimony of Perry Lieber, at the time a vice president of RKO and later an executive of Hughes's Summa Corp. in Las Vegas. He talked with Hughes the next day and verified my story.

I never did find out whether the violinist ever brought out the right girl from the cocktail party.

W. Parkman Rankin is a professor emeritus of the Walter Cronkite School of Journalism at Arizona State University. He has worked as a sales executive for Redbook, This Week, *Time Inc., and Newsweek Inc.*

George C. Wallace

David Dick

On a stormy night in 1968, I first laid eyes on
Alabama's George Corley Wallace, who became my specialty of speciali-
ties. There had been not one, but three presidential campaigns with Governor Wallace, and the storms of those days had probably perverted my
psyche. "They ought to be drilled for the holler horn," was a quick way
for Wallace to insult the intelligence of "long-haired hippies" and at the
same time draw a roar of approval from a crowd of his supporters. A
"holler" (hollow) horn meant not having an ounce of sense.

Baltimore was drenched with a horizontally slanted downpour with
winds whipping the water at gale force. Wallace had arrived on a white-
knuckle flight, and he was staring out of the front starboard window of
the DC-3, muttering to himself and occasionally others, if they'd listen:

"See those clouds ovah thah? Now, he-yuh. Bettah go round those
clouds, y'all he-yuh?"

One of the first people to stomp off Wallace's plane was Sam Donaldson,
who had just begun charging hard for ABC News. Wallace's bodyguards on
the last stop had seized Sam's television crew's footage of the governor shaking hands with the imperial wizard of the Ku Klux Klan. Wallace accused
Donaldson and his crew of waiting for one shot of one handshake in a long
line of handshakes, and the governor said he had ordered the footage seized
to prevent a civil disturbance; Donaldson said it was vintage censorship.

I had followed Wallace from one end of the country to the other, and
if anything I had become too close to him. One time in the Miami area, I
was the only network correspondent with the governor when he showed
up at a huge crowd of Republicans, where he was so popular they almost
ate him for supper. Later in the back seat of the governor's car, Wallace
turned to me and said:

73

"David, what will ah do if ah win the presdency?"

"Well, Govnah, ah guess you'll run the country," were the only words I could think to say.

Sometimes late at night the governor would invite me up to his hotel room on the campaign trail, or I'd invite myself and he'd let me come in. I began to realize that some of the things I said to Wallace were beginning to come back to me in his speeches. That was when I realized I was too close, yet I never complained about it. George Corley Wallace knew how to give a stem-winding, stump-thumping, slung-twice speech a long time before our paths first crossed. There would be times in which I would calculate in advance what the governor might say or do:

"Governor, if I were to say CBS has learned that Governor George Wallace will announce he is going to be a candidate by, say, next week, would that make me look foolish?"

The governor might just smile, or he might say, "Noooooo, I don' think that would make you look foolish, David."

And I would go to a public phone and file a one-minute piece for the radio hourlies, built around the line, "CBS News has learned that Governor George Wallace will announce that he will be a candidate, and the announcement will probably be made next week."

Cameraman Laurens Pierce and I made a conscious decision on our own that we would cover George Wallace in 1972 as if he *were* the President of the United States. Although we frequently didn't agree with him, we would treat him with presidential respect, and we would seldom let him out of our sight. We were there when he turned in for the night, and we were there when he walked out the door first thing in the morning. We stayed with him like white on rice.

We were with Governor Wallace in the Laurel, Maryland, shopping center on May 15, 1972, the day Arthur Bremer fired five bullets at close range, tearing up the governor's insides and leaving him paralyzed for life. The governor had had his favorite hamburger with lots of catsup and French-fries at lunch just before the shooting, which would cause the surgeons at Holy Cross Hospital in Silver Spring to feel like they were gathering pebbles on the moon.

I had looked Arthur Bremer in the eye at the preceding rally in Wheaton, Maryland, and had decided not to attempt to interview him because he looked so weird. I was tired of being accused of talking only to weird-looking people. There were always weirdos following all of the candidates around, but Bremer really looked like a fruitcake. He was plastered with Wallace campaign stickers, buttons, and anything else he could find, and I decided to interview other more respectable-looking disciples. I remembered how bizarre a man Bremer seemed to be at an earlier rally in Hagerstown, Maryland—Bremer down front, applauding with his arms fully outstretched, his hands coming together with sweeping, quick, hard claps. Bremer had cheered, while state police were dragging out black McGovern supporters who had shouted, "Bullshit, Bullshit!" during the opening prayer for the Alabama governor. Hardly anything infuriated Wallace's bodyguards more than for somebody to say "bullshit" while the governor was being prayed over.

It was Laurens Pierce of Montgomery, Alabama, and Atlanta, Georgia, who actually won the Emmy for the coverage of the shooting of Governor Wallace. That footage also resulted in Emmys for Walter Cronkite, Dan Rather, Roger Mudd, and myself. We were called the "team of correspondents" who reported the story on the *CBS Evening News with Walter Cronkite* on May 15, 1972, but without Laurens Pierce's footage there would have been no Emmy for anybody. Pierce had been at the eye of storms, and he was one of those who taught me to be calm in the middle of disaster. If I had been Pierce I would not have remained calm when he of all people was not invited to be a part of the live, nationally televised Emmy Awards night in New York. Pierce appeared earlier with the "technical" staff. The "team of correspondents" enjoyed the live spotlight.

Four years before the Emmy Awards night, I had been in Los Angeles with the Eugene McCarthy presidential campaign when Robert Kennedy was assassinated. I had been sent out to the hospital where the only bridge over troubled waters was the silver bird sent by the Almighty to bring a son home. In the early morning hours I tried to do an on-camera standupper, but I failed miserably, because I had nothing to say. Not even two well-functioning adrenal glands could make my mouth work. I froze. Live. On camera. I never understood why I wasn't fired on the spot. In fact, nobody ever asked about it, and I made sure I never talked to anybody about it. Everybody was in such a state of shock, the network executives may have thought I was understandably and forgivably bereaved. The fact was I had only been with the network two years. I had not been properly prepared at a local affiliate station, and I had not attended a broadcast school that gave degrees in "talking on your feet." I was caught in a storm I didn't understand and no amount of groping or coaching would cause connected words to come out of my mouth. I just made a solemn promise to myself that if ever "my guy" were assassinated I would try to be more professional next time.

On May 15, 1972, I was standing about ten feet from Arthur Bremer. I had already written him off as kook *du jour*. I decided I'd better go to the telephone and advise the CBS Washington bureau at 2020 M Street that if the *CBS Evening News* wanted a piece from me I'd better head in that direction. At the previous rally, protestors had thrown apple cores and chicken eggs at the governor.

"How quiet is the rally where you are?" producer Ed Fouhy asked.

"Very quiet," were the words that would haunt me the rest of my life.

"Then come on in, *if* everything is quiet."

"Everything's quiet. I'm on my way."

I walked past Arthur Bremer again with his silly smile on his face, and I spoke with Pierce, who was rolling on the last of Wallace's "The Speech," the one we had heard so many times we just about had it memorized.

"Cover for me, Pierce," I whispered. "I'm going in to put together a piece for the broadcast."

"Yes, suh," said Pierce in his finest noblesse oblige southern drawl.

I walked past Bremer one more time, found my car on the edge of the rally, and headed toward 2020 M Street. As I turned from Washington Circle near the bureau, an announcer broke in on WTOP radio:

"Governor George Wallace...Laurel, Maryland, shopping center...shots fired...the governor went down...police have arrested the gunman...Wallace's wife, Cornelia, fell down on the governor to try to protect him from being hit again...we'll have more details."

"We'll have more details...we'll have more details...we'll have more details," ricocheted through my brain as I parked the car and jumped out and ran for the building at 2020 M Street. As I was entering the elevator, Marvin Kalb, the state department correspondent for CBS, also stepped on.

"They've shot Governor Wallace," I sputtered.

Marvin's reaction was an expression that said, "Not again."

Laurens Pierce was the only television cameraman rolling on the attempted assassination, and there was blood splattered on Pierce's white trousers. If I had been there I probably would have been hit by one of the bullets, because I always walked immediately behind Wallace's right shoulder. My right arm was usually extended in front of the Governor because I tried to record every word he uttered. Any one of five different parts of the footage could have qualified for an Emmy: the hand extended before the silly smile; the hand with the gun; the "pop, pop, pop, pop, pop" of the pistol; the governor falling to the ground and Cornelia falling on top of him; a bullet grazing the neck of a Secret Service agent; police wrestling to the ground the young man with the silly smile; the bodyguards loading the governor into a station wagon. It was Sy Wolen, Pierce's soundman, who captured the audio of the "pop, pop, pop, pop, pop," and Sy who went to a public telephone and filed a report to CBS Radio. It was Laurens Pierce who commandeered a Singer Sewing Machine delivery truck and handcarried the priceless footage to the CBS Washington Bureau. While the film was in the soup, and everybody prayed it would come out all right, Pierce was interviewed live on the network by Roger Mudd.

On the way to Holy Cross Hospital, I beat my fist on the dashboard. "My guy" had gone down, and I wasn't there to report it. I didn't know how I was going to enter the hospital, because reporters were kept out, so I began walking toward the front door as if I were a "friend of the family." The wife of the Baptist minister, who usually began the rallies with a prayer for the governor, was standing in the entrance with three Maryland state troopers.

"Where have you been, David?" she asked.

"I'm here," I replied as if I were a mourning, long lost cousin.

"A friend of the family," said the woman, nodding to the state troopers. They and the hospital administrators didn't catch on for several days.

It drove Cassie Mackin of NBC to distraction. Often when I would walk through the lobby, Cassie would have her face buried against the glass door. She was not happy with me. One time she waved to me to come closer so she could speak to me.

"Ethics, David," she said. "Ethics."

"Sorry, Cassie," I replied, and kept on being a friend of the family.

Pierce had also gained entrance to the hospital using the same trick. So had Steve Bell of ABC News. One day Pierce and I were in the conference room where "Big Ruby," Governor Wallace's mother-in-law, was stage-managing the incoming floral arrangements. We were up to our patoots in flowers. The telephones on the conference table rang repeatedly.

"Is this Holy Cross Hospital?"

"Yes, it is," Big Ruby, Pierce or I would reply.

"I'd like to get a word to Governor Wallace."

"Why sure, what would that be?"

"Tell him we're praying for him."

"Ah'll be sure he gets the message. Thank you very much for cawlin'."

Miz Ruby (we would never think of calling her by the disrespectful "Big Ruby") knew Pierce and me like she did the back of her hand. She knew we wanted one thing, and that was to be the first cameraman and reporter to gain entrance to Governor Wallace's room. One day, Miz Ruby smiled from ear to ear and said, "Boys, how'djewall like to hep me 'liver these here flairers up to the govnuh's room?"

Pierce and I didn't waste time even looking at one another, much less say anything. We started reachin' fer flairers, big bunches of heavenly flairers, and with grieving looks on our faces, held them close to our hearts. Pierce hid his loaded Bell & Howell silent camera behind one assortment. We were off to the races. We had to cross the lobby directly in front of Cassie and all the others who were not "friends of the family." I looked at them like the rabbit in the battery commercial on television twenty years later. We just kept "going and going and going..."

When we passed Steve Bell, where he was seated talking to an FBI agent, Steve looked up and what he saw he didn't want to believe. Pierce and I pushed the UP button on the elevator, and he and I and Miz Ruby stepped inside. Before the door could close, Steve Bell's frantic face appeared briefly.

"Wh-wh-where are you-you-you all go-go-going?" he stammered.

I said, "Steve, we jes goin' up ta delivah these heah flairers to the guvnah, and if you wanna go, you bettah git some too."

The elevator doors closed and up we went. When we stepped out on the governor's floor, a secret service agent who knew us said, "Where do you think you're going?"

"We gonna delivah these heah flairers to the guvnah's room, ain't thet rite, Miz Ruby?"

"Why, sho," said Miz Ruby.

"No you're not," said the agent. "You're going to sit over there in that waiting room until we figure out what to do about this."

Pierce and I sat down. In about one minute, the elevator door opened again and out stepped ABC News correspondent Steve Bell. He had a pitiful, little, single flower in his hand and a sheepish look on his face. The secret service agent motioned for Steve to join us, about the way a state trooper would flag down a car that had come upon a head-on collision.

"Set down and res' yoself, Steve," I said.

An Alabama state trooper who had traveled with us for two presidential campaigns put on a show for the secret service agent, as it had been done many times before.

"Gimme thet gawddamned camra, Pierce," the trooper snarled, and then winked at Pierce so the secret service agent couldn't see it.

That same afternoon three friends of the family—Laurens Pierce, Steve Bell, and I—were asked to leave the hospital. We did, peacefully, but not until after Pierce had attempted to persuade the trooper to keep the camera and use it to take some pictures for CBS.

"Ah cain't do thet, Pierce, gawddamn."

So, we went outside where Cassie and all the other ethical folks were, and there we stayed for weeks.

David Dick, after retiring from CBS News in 1985, was director of the School of Journalism at the University of Kentucky, where he also was University Orator; he is president of his own publishing company, Plum Lick Publishing, and is the author of The View from Plum Lick *and* Follow the Storm, *where this piece first appeared.*

Green Jelly Beans

Emil Dansker

Dave Hall was mayor of Dayton, Ohio, when I was assigned to city hall for the *Dayton Daily News*. He had histoplasmosis, a debilitating disease of the lungs, and there was no doubt that he would have to resign before his term was up.

But he simply would not talk about it.

In fact, the official words he spoke to me when I met with him after taking the beat were "Daley's a _____ liar!" after I asked him about a speculative column that had appeared in the *Daily News* a few days before.

My city editor had told me in no uncertain terms that when Dave did resign we—the *Daily News*—would get the beat on the story.

Meaning, I would get it for us, or else.

Dave was in and out of the hospital, and on one slow afternoon while he was in, I decided to drive to the hospital to see if I could get someone to take a list of four questions in to him. I knew his room number, but I definitely was NOT going to try to get into the room itself.

Security was especially tight at that hospital, and there was no way I was going to get onto a lobby elevator since I wasn't family. So on the drive down I tried to figure out how I was going to do it.

Finally, it came to me that it was St. Patrick's Day, and I recalled that Dave had quite a sense of humor—I still have a lighter he gave me engraved, "Stolen from the mayor's wife"—and that I would be passing a candy store, so I stopped at the store, bought a bag of green jelly beans, and then went up to the receptionist in the emergency room.

"The Jaycees (I wasn't a Jaycee—Junior Chamber of Commerce—but I had been) thought the mayor would like some green jelly beans for St. Patrick's Day," I said. "Want some?"

She seemed to think that was kind of cute and took some, and I took

80

the emergency room elevator, thus bypassing the nurses' station—I knew a lot about those things because I had been a lay chaplain in a state mental hospital—and was going right to the room.

I had no intention of trying to get into the room, but the nurse, who was serving meals, and who happened to be the mayor's daughter-in-law, agreed to take in the list of questions.

They came back pretty fast with "no comment" to each, but the gimmick broke the ice, and when the mayor finally resigned, the *Daily News* got the beat on the story.

Emil Dansker, Ph.D., has taught journalism at Central State University (Ohio), Bowling Green (Ohio) State University, the University of Cincinnati, Xavier University (Cincinnati), and the University of Dayton. He worked at the Cincinnati Enquirer, *the* Dayton Daily News, *and other publications. He was coproducer of the videotape documentaries "Kent 1970: Covering the Confrontation" and "Expelled from Iran."*

"Stealing" the Stadium Plans

Emil Dansker

I don't remember the year, but it must have been circa 1964 that I was assigned as urban affairs writer for the *Cincinnati Enquirer* to cover the project to build a sports stadium—now Riverfront Stadium—in Cincinnati.

I already had spent a week with the architects in Atlanta—I also was architectural critic for the *Enquirer*—and then came word from my city editor that a model of the proposed stadium was on its way by station wagon from Atlanta and that a team (not including me) would try to meet it along the way to get art.

That didn't work, but I was on hand after the model was placed in a room at the old Sheraton-Gibson Hotel on Walnut Street in Cincinnati for a meeting that night of the oversight committee of government officials and interested private parties, including officials from the Cincinnati Reds.

There was no time to get a photographer over before the doors were locked for a private meeting that night, with a press conference set for the next morning to show the model and to make public the first renderings and the first formal estimates of the cost of the project.

Well, that wouldn't do the *Enquirer,* a morning paper, any good because everybody else would then have the stuff before our next edition.

So, that evening the city editor, the city hall reporter, the art director, a photographer, and I gathered outside the meeting room to buttonhole the participants as they went in, but we got nothing but "no comment" from everyone.

At some point while the meeting was in progress, a young man came by and told me he had left his grey felt hat in the room during the afternoon and asked me if he could go in to get it. I told him it wasn't our meeting, but that I supposed that if he knocked on the door, that they'd let him in; he did, and they did, and he left, pleased to have recovered his hat.

Later, I opined that the participants would have dinner brought in so they could keep working and keep the model secure, so I told the photographer, the late Bob Free, that I would stick my foot in the door to block the serving cart so he could see the model and shoot it.

But the group did move to another room for dinner, leaving us plotting outside the meeting room as to how we could get in to shoot the model.

While we were plotting, a hotel employee in a uniform came up with another man, unlocked the door, went in, and soon came out, relocking the door.

Then I had a hunch: Something told me the hotel guy would come back.

And he did.

After he unlocked the door, I said to Free, "Say, Bob, did you ever get your grey felt hat out of that room?"

Said Bob: "Hat? Oh, yeah, hat!"

And the two of us walked past the hotel man, who said nothing and made no attempt to stop us before he left again.

By this time, the model, which was in a plastic box, was under a sheet with a stack of material on it. I set the stack on a table, pulled off the sheet, and examined the material while Bob fired away, doing what turned out to be beautiful work even through the plastic box—and you know how hard that is in a studio, let alone under those conditions.

The material turned out to be the renderings and cost estimates.

When Bob was finished, I put the sheet and all but two of the sets of material back on the box and we left. The next day at the press conference there was a stack of *Enquirers*—I brought them over myself—with a Page One story reporting what had been presented during the closed meeting the night before.

Two weeks later, another press conference was scheduled—to be held instead at the Netherland Hotel two blocks away because of the security lapse at the Sheraton-Gibson. I told my city editor I doubted I could pull it off again, but I would try.

This was a Sunday, so I dressed in suit and tie and took my two youngest kids for a walk downtown with Daddy.

I knew the room where the press conference was to be held, so we went there, and I was just putting my hand on the doorknob when a man came around a corner and asked, "Could I help you?"

"Oh, I just wanted to see if everything is ready for the meeting tomorrow."

"What meeting is that?"

"The one on the stadium."

"Oh, I doubt it's in there," he said, but he took out his keys and opened the door, and there was the model.

He went on down the corridor while the three of us went inside. As I was writing a note for Alice to run over to the *Enquirer* to get a photographer, I noticed that the paper I was using was a wrapper.

And inside the wrapper were the revisions made following the first meeting.

I was picking up a copy of the material to carry off when the man came in.

"Everything okay?" he asked.

"Yes," I said. "We got what we wanted."

And the next day at the press conference there was a stack of *Enquirers* and...

Postscript: The chairman of the committee came up to me during the morning and said, "I know how you did it last time. How did you do it this time?"

My answer: "No comment."

Emil Dansker, Ph.D., has taught journalism at Central State University (Ohio), Bowling Green (Ohio) State University, the University of Cincinnati, Xavier University (Cincinnati), and the University of Dayton. He worked at the Cincinnati Enquirer, *the* Dayton Daily News, *and other publications. He was coproducer on the videotape documentaries "Kent 1970: Covering the Confrontation" and "Expelled from Iran."*

Go with Your Gut

Gregg Hoffmann

I try to emphasize to my students that they must check their reports, or maps, with the territory. I also stress that the very hierarchy of news organizations makes that difficult to do at times. The fact that editors, who often do not get out on the streets, hold the power to make news judgments too often leads to maps that are based on their assumptions rather than inferences actually drawn from observation or fact-finding in the field.

As an example, I tell a story about the "censored coyote." In the late 1970s, while on the regional staff of a medium-sized daily newspaper in Wisconsin, I worked with another reporter on a nineteen-part series about land use. My editor was lukewarm at best on the series, claiming it would be boring and go virtually unread. "All that zoning and stuff; nobody is interested in that," were his words.

However, I knew from years of covering municipal government that many of the debates and issues faced by local boards centered around how we were to use the land. I also believed the story could be told in a human way. The editor disagreed, but said we could work on the series if we were willing to do it without comp time. We were young and foolish enough to take on the project in our "spare time."

One of the stories I did centered around the effects of development on habitat for wildlife. I spent several days tramping around the bushes with people from the Department of Natural Resources, whose jobs included taking a census of what animals were in those bushes.

These people told me they had counted at least eleven coyotes in southeastern Wisconsin. I did not actually see one during my days with the DNR people, but I had little reason to doubt their word. I also thought it was a significant fact to include in the story, since the presence of coyote

85

and other similar animals indicated that the area had not become entirely urbanized. Animals that were adaptable could still survive, albeit in considerably fewer numbers than the predevelopment rush.

My editor refused to believe coyotes were left in the area, despite the fact I attributed their existence to people who were charged with taking the animal census. My editor had not been off a sidewalk in the last decade of his life, and according to his world, coyote had long been eliminated from our circulation area. He was unable to get beyond his assumptions and would not even make a follow up phone call to the DNR. The coyote reference was taken out of my story.

The stubbornness of this individual, and his unwillingness to draw inferences from what seemed to be verifiable evidence from the field, made me lose considerable respect for him. I eventually took a longtime offer from a competing newspaper in a town ten miles south.

The land use series won a national award from the American Planning Association and drew letters from readers for weeks. The newspaper repackaged it into a tab section. My editor actually had the audacity to try to grab some of the credit.

This story has a couple of lessons for students. First, if you believe in a story enough, be persistent. Even the most closed-minded editors can be swayed in time. Second, a good journalist checks the field, then develops his or her story. The maps are developed from observation and checking the territory. Good editors stay in touch with the territory as much as possible, and don't let their egos and assumptions get in the way of sound news judgment.

I still work part time for that newspaper in the neighboring town. My editors trust my judgment if I can show supporting facts. And I tell the story of the "censored coyote" just about every semester as a reminder that a good journalist checks his maps with his territory.

Gregg Hoffmann is a senior lecturer at the University of Wisconsin-Milwaukee and veteran journalist. His book, Media Maps & Myths, *applies general semantics to news judgment and reporting methods.*

Don't Let Yourself Be Used

Reporters use sources everyday for information, but sometimes sources use reporters—for their own political purposes. When Ron Pruitt got a great tip from a public official, he went after the story, as any reporter would. It wasn't until later that he reali[zed he] had been used to settle a score. He was the pawn that helped a d[istrict] attorney do something he couldn't have done on his own—get rid of [a politic]al enemy. Always question why someone is feeding you inform[ation, t]hen check the facts to see if they warrant rushing into a story, or if [more] time is needed to flesh it out.

Ed Diamond wishes he had checked o[ut some] things before he went to press. He tells us how even an experienc[ed rep]orter can get taken if he's not careful.

And don't think it's only sources wh[o want] to use you. Don Corrigan's story proves reporters can be used even by [their o]wn papers. The women's pages were one area where young reporter[s were] channeled and then ignored. This seems to have improved, but now a [new "w]omen's pages" has sprung up—suburban sections. Many news edit[ors thin]k of zoned editions as second-class journalism and have no intention [of movi]ng reporters from there onto the city desk pages. I found this out when [I was] hired as a metro reporter at a midsized daily. Instead, at the request of the [man]aging editor, I filled an empty slot on a suburban supplement, and then I found out I was being left there to die. I didn't die—I quit, with no job lined up, when I saw that I would never move on. So beware, these beats can be good entry-level positions into a paper, but if you stay awhile and realize they are dead ends, get out.

Finally, Joan Lowenstein tells how she found out what Corrigan and I did—that a reporter has to look out for herself, even in her own newsroom. She stood up for her story because she knew it was right, even though her news director failed to support her. Don't be afraid to fight when you know you're right.

Beware of the
Overhelpful Source

Ron Pruitt

The media is often accused of exploiting people for their news value, but in some instances that situation can be reversed. This incident happened to me when I was the area reporter for the *Muskogee* (Oklahoma) *Daily Phoenix*. I tell this story to illustrate how skillful and manipulative officials use the media to their advantage and to warn students to consider the motivation of those who provide juicy information.

I was making the rounds of the county offices one morning, looking for news, when the district attorney in an adjoining county dropped a bombshell. He said he planned to indict the county sheriff on felony charges. During a short interview in his office the district attorney told me that an audit had revealed shortages in the county fund used to feed the jail's prisoners. Charges of misuse of public funds would be brought against the sheriff.

I realized immediately that I had been handed a big story and pressed for more details. The district attorney said that the paperwork was underway, and he didn't want to comment further, but he said if I returned to my paper and waited he would have more information for me later that day.

Since the district attorney wouldn't talk, I decided to confront the sheriff with the allegation. However, when I arrived at his office, I was told that he would be out until late that day. I left an urgent message for him to call me.

As I drove back to the newsroom, I was excited about the prospect of breaking a big story. I also wondered why the district attorney had chosen me for this honor. I concluded that it was because I had cultivated him carefully over the course of the past few months and because I was the representative of the major newspaper in the area. My self-congratulatory air obscured some other information I should have realized was relevant. The district attorney and the county sheriff were not friends; they had clashed over several issues during the sheriff's first term. In addition, this district attorney had a reputation as a slick politician and a shady wheeler-dealer.

88

I thought about those things, but I was still zealous. The district attorney had been a helpful and reliable source on another big story I had recently done, so I was somewhat inclined to trust him.

When I got back to the paper and told my editors about my impending story, they were excited too, and told me to concentrate on fleshing it out.

The afternoon passed with no further information from the D.A.'s office or from the sheriff, despite my repeated phone calls. I was being stalled, but the D.A. assured me the information was coming.

Finally the county offices closed and I began calling the officials' home numbers. Into the early evening the results were the same—no more information. I was getting frustrated. Finally, about 9 P.M. the D.A. told me he was sending an assistant district attorney to the paper with the information I had been promised. The sheriff was still unreachable. I suspected he was hiding out, and this tended to confirm a growing suspicion that the D.A.'s accusations were valid.

I cooled my heels for another couple of hours and then, finally, at 11:30 P.M. the assitant district attorney arrived at the newsroom. Disappointingly, he brought no paperwork or documentation, but volunteered to be interviewed. I conducted a short interview with him, painfully aware that the paper's deadline was at hand. The assistant D.A. added little to the story, basically repeating the same information his boss had told me earlier. I managed to get a few more quotes and about midnight I frantically typed up my final version of the story. My editors and I discussed the status of the story and, although it was not as thoroughly nailed down as we would have liked, we decided to go with it.

The paper bannered it across the top of the front page the next morning. The wire services picked it up, and it ran in the state's major newspapers the next day as well as on radio and TV.

The sheriff resigned the day the article appeared. No charges were ever brought against him by the D.A. and the new sheriff was much more closely aligned with the D.A.'s office. The D.A. declined any further comment about the whole incident, as did the ex-sheriff.

I should have felt buoyant about breaking such a story. Normally it would have been a coup. But I didn't feel good, I felt used. I had an unsettling feeling that the whole thing had been a power move by the D.A. to dispose of a political enemy, and it apparently had worked to perfection. I had been the unwitting instrument of destruction, a pawn in the game.

Maybe the sheriff had been guilty of taking county money. After all, he resigned. Or maybe he just didn't want to face the embarrassment of the criminal justice process. I never found out the truth since no charges were brought and my sources dried up.

I can say this. My trust in public officials nosedived after that, and I decided that in the future it would be better to lose an important story than to be a participant in a smear campaign. I tell my students not to let their enthusiasm for the big story allow them to be so used.

Ron Pruitt has taught journalism at Pittsburg State University in Kansas. He worked for the Muskogee Daily Phoenix *and as radio news director at KTLQ-AM and KEOK-FM in eastern Oklahoma.*

Even Pros Get Taken

Edwin Diamond

Two cautionary episodes—one early in my reporting career, one recent—not only stand out in my memory but are also extremely useful in my teaching. I share them with my students in an effort to make them aware of the ways of the big bad world out there and of the habits journalists must cultivate.

The first episode occurred in the late 1950s when I was a Washington reporter for the old International News Service, covering defense, science, and national security. Through insider sources at a key military agency, I came across advance information of a major U.S. nuclear initiative that was to be announced by the president of the United States himself in a matter of days. When I checked around in preparation for filing my "world exclusive," word about my story reached top administration figures. One of them—I'll call him "the admiral"—reached me at home one night. I practically stood at attention and saluted when he came on the line: this was the Fifties, after all, and I was thirty years old, making maybe $125 a week (and not too many years out of military service myself). The admiral informed me that premature publication of my story might "jeopardize America's international position." It could harm the president; the initiative itself might be endangered (given the cunning of the president's enemies, both domestic and foreign). I must NOT publish.

The arguments were strong; this was the height of the cold war; our way of life was threatened. Still I hesitated. What about *my* way of life? I had a wife and baby to feed, a career to nourish (oh, yes, there was the people's right to know, as well). I didn't learn journalism on the streets of Chicago for nothing. I bargained with the admiral. I would hold back publication "in the national interest." But when the story was ready for

91

release, he must give me a half-day's lead time—so INS could put the story out on its wire and insure my exclusive. Deal. Truth and INS's clients were served. My brilliant career went forward.

I tell my students that such a scenario would be impossible today. No admiral would make such a call. If he did, it would mean *two* stories, not one. First, the reporter would run an exclusive, on the reasonable assumption that if he or she was able to learn of the initiative, other administration friends or foes would, inevitably, also know. Next, the reporter would do a follow-up on how the government sought to stop publication through nighttime pressures.

The second episode, in the 1990s, involved the late British press lord Robert Maxwell, the week he acquired the *New York Daily News*. It was a major breaking story and I was expanding my media column in *New York* magazine into a cover story about Captain Bob and the *News*. My narrative recounted the *News*'s troubled history, the details of the deal, the governor's role, the unions' reaction to the purchase, Maxwell's background, a rundown of his other media holdings, the New York City newspaper wars, color, quotes, analysis, etc. Absent was a real sense of what Maxwell planned to do with the *News*. My piece was also one-sided, harsh on Maxwell. Even then, I was familiar enough with his reputation to be skeptical. Still, we needed balance; he was saving the paper, wasn't he? Where were his words? It was Wednesday night; Thursday the magazine closed. I talked myself through his press aide into an interview with Maxwell. He must see me ASAP. I would then hustle back to the office and knock out a fast one-page sidebar to the running story, to give some space to his views.

I met him on his 120-foot yacht Thursday at 8 A.M.; a master of the grand gesture, as well as a conniver and a crook (although that wasn't so clear then), he had contrived to have the *Ghislaine* docked at the Water Club on the East River at 32nd Street. In the grand dining room, three aides hovered as I prepared to ask my questions. But first he had some business calls to make. As his secretary fed him names and numbers, he called various bigwig merchants and CEOs around the city. Naturally I listened and made mental notes as Maxwell asked/coaxed/affirmed that Modell's, Bloomingdale's, Macy's, Potamkin Cadillac, etc. would be advertising again in the *News*. The calling done, the interview proceeded. I went back and wrote the sidebar, including touches from the overheard calls. The piece closed on time.

A year later, he went overboard off the stern of the *Ghislaine* into the Atlantic waters around the Azores. A body said to be Maxwell's was later recovered. The Maxwell empire took a dive as well; the *News* came under the protection of bankruptcy court. Writing that final chapter for *New York*, I began to wonder just how crooked he had been with me. Those phone calls, for example. Remarkable, wasn't it, that at eight in the morning he was able to reach so many important executives at their desks, immediately, and just as quickly was able to MAKE THE SALE. Or was it all a dumb show, for my benefit? Was anyone actually on the other end of the line? The secretary, the aides, everyone would have had to be in on the scam, and for what? Could they be so sure I'd take the bait, listen in, and write about how effective Maxwell was (the *News* was back!)? Could they count on me, strapped by deadlines, not to call Modell's, Macy's, et al., to see if they actually were coming back to advertise in the *News?* Were those phone calls real? My readers were led to believe they were. To this day, though, I'll never know for sure.

Lesson: Verify, don't trust. You can have forty years in the business under your belt—wire services, newspapers, news weeklies, magazines, prize-winning books, and be a critic and teacher of journalism—and still get taken.

Edwin Diamond, a critic and journalism professor at New York University, is author of ten books on politics and media. He began his reporting career at the Chicago American *in 1953. His most recent book,* Behind the Times: Inside The New York Times, *was published by Villard Books in 1994. The University of Chicago Press planned to bring out the paperback edition, with epilogue, in summer 1995.*

Joining the Women's Pages

Don Corrigan

I began my career as a reporter in the 1970s, and was part of the bulge of journalism school students attributed to Watergate. We were all looking for a piece of that drama and excitement which propelled Woodward and Bernstein to national fame. My last semester of graduate study was on the Mizzou J-School's London Reporting Program, and I fully expected to be hired by a major metro daily upon graduation for work as a James Bond-type international correspondent investigating oil cartels, coups d'etat and U.S. foreign policy fiascoes.

Several months and hundreds of newspaper rejection letters after J-School graduation, I finally landed a job on the *Bloomington Daily Pantagraph.* Covering the odd-named hamlets that interrupt the crazy quilt of corn fields in central Illinois, *Pantagraph* stories seldom merited national attention.

Watergate wasn't the only phenomenon to hit the journalism industry in the 1970s. Something called the women's movement also was reshaping the news: That section called the "Women's Pages" was suddenly being transformed into "Scene," "Tempo," "Style," and "Family Living;" that section also was being integrated with male staffers.

At the *Pantagraph,* I was offered a chance to join the revolution and to become the first male reporter on the newly-designed "Living Today." My reasons for accepting the challenge had less to do with any ambition to be on the cutting edge of journalism and much more to do with the hours. If I signed up with "Living Today," I would have a regular eight-hour shift during the day. Otherwise, I would be "working tonight," listening to the police scanner and chasing fire engines until well after midnight.

Since I had worked for, and with, plenty of women journalists on the *Columbian Daily Missourian* at the University of Missouri, I really didn't give my choice of duties at the *Pantagraph* a second thought. But Bloomington, Illinois, in the late 1970s was lagging behind the enlighted attitudes of journalism practiced in academia. I soon learned that my fellow male Pantagraphers had a lot of second thoughts about a guy who would voluntarily enter the second-class purgatory of the women's pages— no matter what kind of fancy name camouflaged the indignity.

At the *Pantagraph,* I was not invited out for a drink with the guys until several weeks after I joined the paper, and then only as an object of curiosity. At the interrogation session over thirty-five-cent Budweiser drafts, I was hit with a barrage of questions: "Was it true that I volunteered to write with the women?" "How could I look myself in the mirror every morning as I prepared for the work of writing news about nuptials?" For some of the old-timers who never attended college, the fact that I volunteered for the women's section just confirmed their suspicions that academia was ruining journalism.

"You know, Corrigan," said one sympathetic fellow, "you seem to be a regular guy. When we heard some guy was going to work with the women's section, we figured he had to be some sort of a fish."

I soon began to feel like "some sort of a fish." I got a good taste of the second-class treatment women have often received in newsrooms since they were first allowed to enter that sacred domain as the "sob sisters" of William Randolph Hearst and Joseph Pulitzer.

Our section was housed in a glass cage next door to the offices of the editor and managing editor. The proximity allowed the paper's patriarchs to conveniently put a lid on "the girls," if there was too much gabbing and the engagement announcements weren't getting typed fast enough. Unlike the fellows in the newsroom, the girls got a scrupulously-timed half hour for lunch. The assumption was that the women would fritter and dally if left to their own devices. By contrast, the newsroom males could take as much time as they needed for lunch, since they were probably out discussing important, late-breaking stories on the city or state desk.

I found myself caught in a bind one day when I went to lunch with the guys and had to leave prematurely to scurry back to "Living Today" in a timely fashion. "We're not through here yet," said the ringleader of a roundtable assessment of a "bodacious brunette" just hired as a summer intern. "What's-a-matter, Corrigan? Got to get together some new recipes this afternoon?"

Attempts at serious journalism were nipped in the bud. My editor would submit such story ideas for review to the patriarchs next door, and they would promptly remind her that "Living Today" is still the "women's pages." She suffered her biggest setback when Rosalynn Carter came to Bloomington, and naturally she expected her section reporters to get the assignment to cover the First Lady's visit. At the last minute, the story was stolen by a city desk editor who argued that Rosalynn belonged to his front page.

I sometimes got into trouble with my female colleagues for not carrying my share in producing wedding copy or covering the vacation tales of "high society" couples. One week I tried to make up for it by bringing back to the newspaper some novel African recipes for fried Dodo and Mosa—a sidebar story to my coverage of a Nigerian delegation visiting Illinois State University. The guys in the newsroom promptly named me "Donita," and thereafter would frequently stick their heads into the "Living Today" cage, asking, "Hey, Donita, got any good recipes for fried Dodo?"

Needless to say, Donita soon began looking for a job that afforded a little more self-esteem. I found two—as a college teacher and a weekly feature editor in a southwest suburb of Chicago. On the afternoon I left "Living Today," my editor apologized for some of the treatment I had received at the hooves of the chauvinistic pigs on the paper. I assured her that no irreparable harm had been done, and that I looked on much of my ordeal as humorous. At that point, she looked at me with great disappointment, as if I were part of the problem and not part of the solution to the status of women in journalism. She reminded me that as a male, I could take the second-hand treatment on the women's pages more lightly because the escape hatch was always open for me.

Since my trial in the late 1970s as the first male on the women's pages of the *Pantagraph*, I'm certain we've all had our consciousness raised in the news business. Women are no longer found primarily writing ninety-five-ways-to-make-tuna-casserole news. Many newsrooms have an equal number of female and male journalists. The content and status of those thinly-veiled women's pages has improved, along with the status of the writers who put them together. That isn't to say there aren't miles yet to travel. And, that's not to say that newsroom offices don't still harbor female-phobic males with attitude problems.

To remind me of just how deeply entrenched those attitude problems can be, I have preserved a letter from a male *Pantagraph* colleague that I received months after leaving "Living Today." His "humorous" letter was in response to the first issue of a weekly newspaper I started with some friends in a Chicago suburb, which I had forwarded to the *Pantagraph* for critical review. It reads:

"As a practicing journalist and former president of the highly respected SDX chapter at Southern Illinois University, I must say that I am appalled at the lack of veracity in the very first edition of this newspaper.

"The gall of one particular member of your editorial staff is enough to knock the journalistic code back several years. . . Of what do I write?

"I quote from a summary of the qualifications of one Don Corrigan who serves as feature editor. '...he later spent a year as a member of the editorial staff at the *Bloomington Pantagraph.*'

"I thought it was a simple coincidence and perhaps another Don Corrigan had once held a position of merit with our newspaper. But no, the mug shot (and I use the term literally) adorning the column erased all hope of your paper's credibility.

"For the record, the closest Corrigan got to the editorial department was the day he was walking by the office and one of his engagement forms floated out of his fish-like hands and under the door. A secretary kindly handed it back to him, through the mail slot, and he shuffled back to his desk in the women's department.

"Yes, Don Corrigan, who now poses as a real member of the working press, was merely an employee of the women's department or, to quote the words of the editor of that department, 'He was an experiment that failed.'

"Corrigan was a purveyor of panty hose, an editor of engagement announcements. Only, let's face it, folks, Corrigan couldn't make it on his own. He didn't even know what a double-ring ceremony was. (He thought it was a Eubangie ritual, one for the finger, one for the nose.)

"Not only has he apparently falsified his records, Corrigan has evidently had his facial features reconstructed. He was never that cute when he was working here. Of course, he just didn't have the figure for gaucho pants.

"As a member of the working press, I would like to see competition among the media thrive and wish well to all sapling ventures. But you're doomed, *Free Press.* Doomed by Don Corrigan.

"Sincerely,

"A Well-Wisher

"P.S. Donita, can I have your recipe for Fried Dodo?"

Don Corrigan is a journalism professor at Webster University in St. Louis, MO, and editor and publisher of Webster/Kirkwood Times *and* South County Times.

A Cautionary Tale

Joan H. Lowenstein

As a reporter, you can get in trouble even when you do everything right. I was working at a television station in Oklahoma City. I was only twenty-two, having come to the station right out of Missouri Journalism School. After being there about a year, I figured I had done a good job and earned both the trust and the loyalty of my superiors. But there is more to learning the news business than just mastering the inverted pyramid.

My beat was the courts, and that included a lot of reporting about crime, arrests, and police activity. The assignment editor sent me out with a photographer to report on what was then (1979) an unusual story. A bus driver from a church-run vacation Bible school had been arrested and charged with sexually molesting children from the school.

The photographer and I headed for the courthouse for the man's arraignment. There, we were met by family members who tried to shield the man and at one point even pushed the camera and the photographer. It was a distasteful news story, and it was even more distasteful to be condemned for just reporting the news, but we went on to finish by interviewing families of the children and then going out to the church to photograph the scene. No one from the church would talk to us and they all but kicked us off the property.

It had been an early-morning story and we got the package together for the noon newscast, a feat that was somewhat amazing in the days of film, when the film had to be developed and edited in time. The photographer and I were proud of having covered a difficult story, reporting it accurately and making our deadline.

Shortly after the piece ran, the news director found me at my cubbyhole in the newsroom. He told me the station manager wanted to see me about the child molestation story. I wondered why I, a lowly reporter, was being asked for a command performance before the station's highest manager, but I didn't say anything and walked up to his office, a place where I had never been. The news director did not accompany me.

After talking on the phone to a few business associates as though I was not in the room, the station manager turned to address me. He asked why, in my story, I had identified the church where the bus driver was employed. I was dumbfounded. He went on to say that the church officials were angry that the church had been identified. He, himself, didn't see any reason why it needed to be identified for the story.

This was amazing to me. I was being called on the carpet for reporting a news story accurately. More amazing was that a busy station manager would bother with such a trivial story and that the news director would not support me or even come with me to respond. There had to be more to this, but, if there was, I never found out.

I asked the station manager how he would feel as a parent of a child in vacation Bible school to hear on the news that "some" bus driver from "some" vacation Bible school had been arrested for molesting children. Had I been a little older and more mature, I think I would have used very indelicate terms, just for effect. He harrumphed and that was the end of our interview.

I never really regained trust in my news director because I felt I had been betrayed. He was unwilling to suffer the wrath of the station manager and it was easier to sacrifice me. In the news business, you have to look out for yourself and stand up for your stories—if they're right.

Joan H. Lowenstein is a lecturer in the communication department of the University of Michigan. She received a journalism degree from the University of Missouri and a law degree from the University of Florida. Lowenstein worked as a television reporter at KTVY-TV in Oklahoma City, specializing in media law. After practicing in firms in Miami and Detroit, she began teaching classes in media law at the University of Michigan. She has won a Michigan Bar Association award for her legal column in the Ann Arbor News *and is a recipient of a Freedom Forum grant.*

Occupational Hazards

In practically every journalism course I have ever taught, students ask about using tape recorders. They seem surprised when I tell them that I never used one when working as a reporter. I always found it quicker and easier to take notes, especially since most of my experience was on daily newspapers, and it would have been nearly impossible to transcribe tapes while on deadline each evening. This is the only way I have ever worked, and, therefore, it is what I feel most comfortable with, so I continue, even as a freelance writer with much more liberal deadlines.

While at least one study has concluded that reporters who use tape recorders produce stories which are no more accurate than stories which have been written from notes only, I have found that professional journalists tend to feel strongly committed to either note-taking or taping, depending on what they are used to. I say, go with whatever makes you more comfortable because that will make the interview—and your story—turn out better. Either way has advantages and disadvantages, as several of our writers here learned.

Sylvan Fox's experience left him firmly convinced that nothing substitutes for a recording of a quote in the source's own voice. Tom Wheeler and Louise Montgomery thought that too until they learned that having a tape recorder and planning to rely only on it can be a mistake.

Not all occupational hazards involve tape recorders, of course. One that seems to plague interns and new reporters in particular is getting caught between editors with conflicting opinions. Pete Benjaminson shares his story of being sent out by one editor and reporting back to another.

Wheeler's second account here doesn't happen too often, because most of our work isn't translated for foreign publications on a regular basis. But when it is, some things can get lost in the translation.

There's No Proof Like a Tape

Sylvan Fox

Only journalists (and possibly brain surgeons) can fully empathize with the gut-wrenching experience of being accused of committing a felonious error. Like surgeons, journalists cannot erase an error; they must either live with it or prove no mistake had been made.

And living with it is not an easy prospect. I can remember misspelling the word sherbet (or is it sherbert?) several times in a story I wrote while I was on a tryout at the old *New York World-Telegram & Sun.* I was sure, when I realized what I had done, that sherbet had spelled the end of my newspaper career.

And shortly after I had joined the staff of *The New York Times,* I incorrectly identified the relationship of a survivor to the deceased in a short obituary I had written. Fortunately, I caught that one between the first and second editions of the paper, and almost nobody noticed.

These were bad enough. But on those occasions, happily rare, when I was charged with the more serious crime of misquoting someone or getting a major fact wrong, I suffered all the awful symptoms of the worst kind of anxiety attack: profuse sweating, a vertiginous sensation, and, if the situation wasn't quickly resolved, acute insomnia. The symptoms intensified or abated depending on the gravity of the offense, but no error, no matter how minor, could be shrugged off without some physical and emotional pain. Even when an accusation was false, and I was completely innocent of any miscreance, I suffered all the pangs of guilt until I had proven, to my satisfaction and my accuser's, that I was entirely blameless.

During thirty-five years in the newspaper business as a reporter, rewriteman, and editor, I probably suffered these terrible travails, whether deservedly or not, perhaps eight or ten times—but never worse than in the spring of 1969 at the City College of New York.

I was covering a major campus uprising at the college for *The New York Times*. It was the usual 1960s sort of affair: students—in this case black and Puerto Rican students demanding, among other things, the establishment of a School of Black and Puerto Rican Studies—had disrupted the City College campus and forced the institution to shut down. Ugly, violent confrontations had occurred between black and white students and the president of the college, Buell Gallagher, had resigned and been replaced by Joseph J. Copeland, a wimpish-looking botanist who was then sixty-one years old and who seemed peculiarly ill-suited to the job under the chaotic circumstances.

A short time after taking office, the new acting president decided to make himself available to the press at a formal news conference. I was assigned to cover it.

At the appointed hour, I entered the world of typical news conference madness. Copeland, looking even more fragile and besieged than usual, sat at one end of a long conference table, and the reporters, photographers, and television technicians crowded around the rest of the table furiously taking notes, switching television lights on and off, and hurling questions at him.

After the news conference had ended, I went down to the *Times* offices on West 43rd Street and wrote my story. Before leaving the office at around 8 P.M., I took a quick look at the dummy of that night's page one and noted with appropriate satisfaction that my account of the Copeland news conference and City College developments was scheduled for prominent display on the front page. And so, with the distinct feeling that I had spent my day well, I cleaned off my desk and headed uptown to my apartment on the Upper East Side, where I had a relaxing drink and dinner with my wife. By 10:30 I was in bed, weary from a long day of covering the City College story and writing a lengthy and complex story afterward.

Half an hour later, my bedside phone rang. It was an assistant editor on the *Times* metropolitan desk who sounded a little tense as he informed me that Israel Levine, the City College public relations chief, had called with a bit of a problem.

Oh, I responded, trying to remain cool. What was the problem?

Levine, the desk editor explained, was complaining that my story, which was predicated on some comments Copeland had made during the news conference, was completely wrong because I had misquoted the acting president. Levine had told the desk editor that Copeland never said what I quoted him as saying and had demanded that my story be yanked out of the subsequent editions.

To the eternal credit of the *Times'* mechanisms for dealing with such grim situations, the desk man called me rather than panicking and taking some kind of radical action. After hearing his report on the conversation with Levine, I explained that I had the challenged quotes in my notes and that I stood by the story. Under the circumstances, I argued, we should concede nothing to Levine until we had explored the situation a lot further the following day. I assume the desk editor reported all this to the metropolitan editor, Arthur Gelb, and that Gelb agreed with our course of action, although I never asked.

Despite my confidence that justice would prevail and that I would be completely exonerated, I lay awake long, uncomfortable hours that night before falling into a brief and fitful sleep.

In the morning, I wasted no time getting up to City College. As I rode uptown in a cab, I already had formulated a plan of action: I would look for someone who had a tape recording of the news conference; that was the only way I could prove beyond a shadow of a doubt that my reporting had been accurate.

By this point in the City College protest, I had become acquainted with a fair number of students of various political and ethnic persuasions. So I started asking every kid I ran into that morning whether he or she knew who had tape-recorded the Copeland press conference the day before. In a remarkably short time, one student said he knew somebody who had taped the conference and within minutes we had found the chubby young man, hauled him into an office and turned on his tape recording.

I sat at a typewriter while we listened to the recording, and when we came to the passage I allegedly had misquoted, I typed verbatim off the tape. Each word filled me with pleasure as I transcribed it, for it was precisely what I had taken from my notes and used in my story. Word for word. Without so much as a single deviation. Even the kid who had made the tape available to me was beaming.

After completing the transcription of the challenged quote, which ran perhaps five or six typewritten lines, I took the paper out of the typewriter, rose triumphantly and strode into Israel Levine's office with the precious typescript in my hand.

"Here Irv," I said, handing him the paper. "I typed this directly off a tape of yesterday's press conference."

Without a word, he took the piece of paper, turned and walked into Copeland's office.

Ten minutes or so later, the man who just a few hours earlier had demanded that a story be pulled from the front page of *The New York Times* emerged looking a little sheepish. Apparently he and Copeland had compared my typed version of the quotes with their own transcription or tape recording of the news conference and not surprisingly had found them identical.

"Well. . .?" I asked, half expecting an apology of some kind. I got none.

Instead Levine looked over at me and said with a completely straight face: "Well, anyway, that's not what he meant to say."

"Irving," I replied a little impatiently. "*The New York Times* pays me to be a reporter. Not a mind reader."

Everywhere I've taught journalism—at NYU, Baylor University and Long Island University—at least one student has asked me whether I thought reporters ought to use tape recorders to capture the remarks of the people they're writing about.

That's when I usually whip out the City College anecdote to emphasize my conviction that there really is no substitute for a record of the quotes you're using in a story. With people's own voices uttering the words a reporter has attributed to them, they're not likely to get very far in claiming to have been misquoted.

However, a few words of caution have to be added to my endorsement of the tape recorder as a journalistic tool. First, a reporter must also take complete and accurate written notes; tape recorders have been known to break down or batteries to have exhausted themselves at inopportune times. Second, a reporter has to ascertain when the presence of a tape recorder, no matter how unobtrusive, inhibits an interviewee from speaking freely. If that becomes a problem, the tape recorder obviously ought to be shut off and stowed somewhere out of sight.

But in most settings, like a crowded press conference at a college under siege, a tape recording can be a life-saver. I tremble to think of the sleepless nights I would have spent back in the spring of 1969 if a jolly young student—whose name I'm not sure I ever had the time to obtain—hadn't made one available to me.

Sylvan Fox has taught at New York University, Baylor University, and Long Island University. He worked for the Little Falls (NY) Evening Times, *the* Schenectady (NY) Union Star, *the* Buffalo Evening News, *the* New York World Telegram & Sun, *where he won a Pulitzer Prize,* The New York Times, *and* Newsday. *He is the author of* The Unanswered Questions About President Kennedy's Assassination.

No Tapes

Tom Wheeler

Going into my interview with Chuck Berry, idol of my youth, I was pumped and well prepared. Or so I thought. I had assembled my gear with the precision of a paratrooper—testing the extra batteries, labeling the cassettes, even packing an extra hand-held recorder. I knew that Chuck could be volatile. His manager warned me that if I made the wrong move or said the wrong word, the interview could be cut short or might not happen at all.

We seemed to hit it off well enough, at least for the first sixty seconds. I unpacked my clipboard, set my recorder on the table, and—"No tapes," he commanded, suspiciously eyeing the little Panasonic. Knowing he distrusted journalists, I launched into a prepared explanation of how the recorder would only increase the story's accuracy, and help ensure clarity, and blah blah blah, but his logic dictated that taping our conversation would somehow only give me more opportunities to distort it, and he would have none of it. "I don't have to do this interview," he reminded me.

There was only one thing to say. "No problem! I'll just take notes!" I wondered if my cheerful demeanor masked my panic. I had conducted scores of interviews and had recored every single one. It had never occurred to me not to. Why slow things down with handwriting? Why interrupt the eye contact? What if there's a disagreement about a published quote and you need proof? Tapes, the only way to go. This time, though, it was take notes or go home. The only problem: no paper. I ransacked my gear, but there were precious few writing materials amid the electronics. It took only fifteen minutes to fill the margins of my question sheets, and I spent the next hour acting like scribbling on cocktail napkins was the most natural thing in the world. After I got home I stayed up till dawn, deciphering my chicken scratches as best I could, reconstructing sentences, filling gaps.

That experience taught me that our subjects don't approach interviews with our kind of agenda or even our kind of logic. I also learned that to be truly prepared, I had to ask myself not only what is likely to go wrong but what can conceivably go wrong.

Tom Wheeler is the author of The Guitar Book *and* American Guitars *(both Harper & Row) and the former editor of* Guitar Player *magazine. He is an associate professor at the School of Journalism and Communication at the University of Oregon, where in 1993 he won the Marshall Award for innovative teaching.*

My Date with Hugh Hefner

Louise Montgomery

My date with Hugh Hefner back when he was the ultimate playboy gives me a guaranteed audience for at least one important lesson in reporting. As time has passed, I realize that my experience, limited as it was, teaches other lessons. So as long as the name *Playboy* and its creator are a part of the popular culture, my story will be useful in teaching journalism students a number of lessons.

To avoid giving away the punch line, I'll let the lessons reveal themselves as I tell the story.

At the *Miami Herald* I created a weekly feature for the Broward Edition called "Celebrity Line" before the concept of reader-friendly had emerged and before most people in the newsroom paid conscious attention to what readers wanted. "Celebrity Line," pioneered by the *Herald*'s sister newspaper, the *Detroit Free Press*, allowed readers to write or record their questions for a celebrity. I interviewed the celebrity, using readers' questions and some of my own.

For the week of April 20, 1969, our celebrity was Hugh Hefner, then unmarried and the focus of many newspaper and magazine articles on his stable of starlets. Questions poured in the five days before the interview. Nineteen sixty-nine was near the peak of the sexual revolution, and Hefner in silk pyjamas was its most visible leader through his free-love lifestyle and his monthy advice column, "The Playboy Philosophy."

I'd arranged to interview him by telephone on Friday afternoon in one of the glass-walled offices at the *Herald*'s Fort Lauderdale office. I set up the tape recorder with a new tape, tested the tape to make sure it and the machine worked, attached the telephone-pickup suction cup to the top of the phone, near the ear. My coworker, Rita Winer, telephoned me from another office to make sure everything worked. Half the newsroom of about forty people gathered outside the office as I placed the call at the arranged time. Just as I'd hoped, Hefner's secretary put the call directly through to him.

From the moment Hefner picked up the phone, the interview sparkled. I'd ask a question, he'd answer with a quip. I'd respond, and he'd continue. We laughed, we bantered and we talked seriously. At the end of ninety mintes, with even more of my coworkers gathered outside the door and windows, I thanked Hefner and hung up the phone.

As soon as the phone hit the cradle, the gallery rushed in. I reached over to rewind the tape recorder. No whirr of tape rewinding. Nothing happened. I panicked and started checking out each part of the machine. The tape recorder hadn't been plugged in. Apparently the batteries had had enough power to make the test, and the recorder had been unplugged. The cause, at that moment, didn't matter. I had nothing of the scintillating interview.

To make matters worse, I'd been enjoying my one and only date with Hugh Hefner so much that I made not one single note. What to do? I had no choice. I dialed his number once more, explained to his secretary what had happened, and Hugh came back on the line immediately. He graciously agreed to do the interview again. So my second date with Hugh Hefner went on for an hour. This time, the recorder was plugged in.

Through the years, I've recounted this story innumerable times to my journalism students, urging them to always make notes, even if they are taping an interview or speech. Each time I've told the story, I've lamented that the second interview was a letdown after the sparkling first run-through.

Now, as I write the story, I am not sure that my lamentations were justified. True, asking the same questions a second time meant the element of surprise was gone. But it was hard to surprise Hefner. I'm sure he'd been asked everything that I asked him in the interview. Hefner proved himself to be an endlessly creative person; instead of repeating the quips from the first interview, sometime he gave new ones. And in the second interview, I was able to follow up on quips that had so dazzled me in the first interview that I hadn't followed up as I should have.

Looking back at the interview more than a quarter-century later, I'm amazed at how lacking in salacious content the interview was. Sure, interviewing a sex god for a daily newspaper meant that we'd stay on safe turf. Even so, looking back at the interview, it's hard to see why traditionalists could have been so alarmed. Here, using questions from readers, is how the published Hefner interview began:

> Q: Don't you ever get tired of just women and women and more women? (Judy)

A: Well, no. My life is a great deal more than just women. I have to work, too. That remains a continuing challenge, and so do women.

The question implies that I'm, well...(a playboy?)...well, yes. I'll plead only partially guilty to that. I'm also very romantic and sentimental.

Q: What do you look for in a woman? (B.G.I.)

A: Honesty, sincerity. I like a person who's direct, open, vulnerable, sensitive. What really turns me off is the pseudo-sophistication that passes for sophistication in some quarters. And competitive females, ones that aren't happy they're women, the ones who think they're guys.

Hefner contrasted his magazine to more graphic magazines but argued against censorship. "A great deal of what is published today is tasteless, but it should not be suppressed," he said. "We can afford a society with tasteless aspects. We can't afford a society that doesn't have a free press." He also supported the Smothers brothers, whose show network TV officials had cancelled because of content deemed too sexy. "TV suffers instead from the bland leading the bland, a lack of decent ideas, lack of variety," Hefner said.

Apart from the obvious lesson that his experience teaches about making sure electronic equipment is working and making notes, even after you've allegedly tested the equipment, I use it to talk about interviewing. Hefner, as you might expect, used my questions as a cue for a clever response. The sixty-minute interview was reduced to about sixty inches of copy. My chore was to decide how many of my readers' questions to publish and how much of Hefner's playfulness to use.

Sometimes journalists become so smitten with their subjects, particularly when they're rich and famous, that they lose sight of the readers' interest. It's easy to let the subject take over the interview, talking only about what he or she wants to talk about. The reporter then has no choice but to write the subject's story, not necessarily the story that the reporter had in mind or wanted. That can work as long as the reporter can cajole or otherwise interest the subject in saying something other than what has been previously published. What's better, in my view, is that the reporter control the interview, allowing the subject to run with the line as long as interesting, useful material is produced, but reeling in if the material becomes stale.

In my case I was protected from losing control of the interview because I had questions from readers that I was determined to pose to Hefner. Having a list of questions is a good practice under all circumstances. Journalists, particularly the inexperienced, aren't immune to stage fright when interviewing famous people. Having a list of questions written out in advance provides security and helps insure that the reporter covers all the material he or she wants.

My interview with Hefner also points up the importance of backgrounding. In the period immediately before I interviewed Hefner, *Time* magazine had done a highly publicized interview with him. Several of our readers had read *Time*'s piece and wanted his comments on it. I, too, read the article and was prepared to follow up on his responses. Similarly, I was familiar with the controversy over the firing of the Smothers brothers. To have interviewed one of the most famous figures in popular culture on the heels of the Smothers' dismissal without asking his comment on it would have been an embarrassing oversight.

Apart from those lessons, the Hefner interview also teaches how easy it is to interview someone who's interesting and who knows what "the media" want. By the time I interviewed him, Hefner had been interviewed thousands of times, and he had interviewed many people. He knew the rules of journalism and what made a good quote, and he played the game well. My task was little more than to pose the topic, and let him respond. Editing the text required little more than putting paragraph marks on it.

At the time I interviewed Hefner, he had the reputation of being hard to reach for an interview. Much has changed in the last thirty years in Hef's life. The King Bunny married one of his playmates and fathered a couple of children. In 1985 he suffered a stroke that hastened the changes that had already begun to occur in his life, his interests, his activities. Now instead of bunnies wearing high heels, the bunnies at the Playboy Mansion are four-legged and naturally furry. But one thing has remained constant. At a time when many of his accomplices in the sexual revolution have joined Accuracy in the Media and similar aggressively conservative organizations, Hef remains true to his philosophy. And I have no doubt that he'd answer most of my questions today just as he did in 1969.

Louise Montgomery, a journalism professor at the University of Arkansas, is spending the 1995–96 academic year as a visiting fellow at Wolfson College, Cambridge University, to research a book on press and government over the last two hundred years. She has worked for the Miami Herald *and* Dallas News, *wrote* Journalists on Dangerous Assignments: A Guide to Staying Alive *for the International Press Institute in London, and had a Fulbright Lectureship in Chile in 1989 to teach investigative reporting.*

First Day

Peter Benjaminson

In case my students think journalism is all glamor, I like to start each semester's class by telling them about my first day in big-time journalism. I was an intern on the mighty *Los Angeles Times*. On my first day there, after I'd sat around the city room reading the paper for about two hours, an assistant city editor called me over.

"A set of 4-year-old triplets was killed in a traffic accident in Antelope Valley the other day. The funeral's today. You go out with Ed here," he said, gesturing to a photographer. "He'll get the shot, you do the caption."

My first assignment! Breathless with excitement, I walked with Ed to his car. I talked nonstop on the two-and-one-half-hour drive to Antelope Valley. He seemed concerned mostly about getting the mileage for the trip right so he would be paid every cent of his reimbursement.

The assignment was an adventure, but not exactly what I had envisioned. The three little white caskets were lined up at the cemetery all right, pretty as a picture. The problem was that the triplets' relatives, who were out in force for the funeral, didn't want the picture taken. Since I was bigger than Ed and he had the camera to handle, I was assigned the job of preventing the relatives from disrupting Ed in his work. While he circled the coffins, shooting—the funeral hadn't started yet—I blocked, in regulation football style, the weeping relatives who ran at him. They were hoping to throw off his aim and ruin his photo.

He finally got a decent picture and we left; I got the caption info from the undertaker, who had remained scrupulously neutral during the mêlée.

The ride out had been easy. On the way back, however, we were caught in rush hour, and the return drive took four hours. We had spent the whole day on this assignment, my first ever in professional newspapering.

111

We finally got back to the *Times-Mirror* building, drenched with sweat. I raced up to the city room to do my precious caption, while, Ed raced for the darkroom to develop his photo. Within twenty minutes, we'd delivered photo and caption to the desk, but we'd taken so long getting back that the editor who had assigned it to us had gone for the day. His replacement took one look at the technically perfect, but sociologically ghastly, photo of the three little coffins and threw both caption and photo in the wastebasket.

"Who sent you out on that?" he said, and turned away.

Peter Benjaminson has worked for Redwood City Tribune, *the* Los Angeles Times, *the* Atlanta Journal, *and the* Detroit Free Press. *He has been a journalism professor at the State University of New York at Binghamton, New York University, and the Graduate School of Journalism at Columbia University. He is the coauthor of* Investigative Reporting *and author of* The Story of Motown *and* Death in the Afternoon: America's Newspaper Giants Struggle for Survival. *Benjaminson is now assistant editor of the* Chief-Leader, *New York City's civil service newspaper.*

Lost in Translation

Tom Wheeler

The late guitar hero Michael Bloomfield was one of those interviewees journalists dream about—colorful, soulful, chatty. After one of our conversations I joked to colleagues that you could just set a tape recorder in front of him, leave the room, come back in an hour, and he would take care of everything.

I had asked Michael about the challenge of living with his past. He then toured as a solo artist, performing intimate tunes on acoustic guitar in small clubs, and yet audiences sometimes expected him to recreate his rock band's electrified hits all by himself.

"I'm the same way," he told me. "I want to see B. B. with a process."

It was Michael's way of saying that he emphasized with his audiences, that when he saw his own hero, B. B. King, in concert he imagined him the way he looked decades before, with the shiny, straightened hairdo popular among African-Americans in the 1950s.

Months later, we allowed the German magazine *Fachblatt* to republish the Bloomfield interview. No one thought to ask to proof the translation. None of us knew a lick of German anyway.

It may have been obvious to our readers the "B. B." referred to B. B. King, but in Europe the initials had for decades referred to someone even more famous. Imagine my surprise when I saw that *Fachblatt*'s editors had taken the liberty of changing "B. B." to "Brigitte Bardot." I suppose that not a lot of harm was done, but I always wondered what those German readers thought of Michael Bloomfield's desire to see Brigitte Bardot with a processed hairdo.

Tom Wheeler is the author of The Guitar Book *and* American Guitars *(both Harper & Row) and the former editor of* Guitar Player *magazine. He is an associate professor at the School of Journalism and Communication at the University of Oregon, where in 1993 he won the Marshall Award for innovative teaching.*

chapter eight

Doing the Best Under
Difficult Circumstances

Being on the scene of a major story can be exciting, but it can also be baffling. Just because a reporter is there doesn't mean he or she always knows what's going on. Jim Featherston and Larry Day found out that sometimes all you can do is just keep asking questions, find out all that you can and report what you know. And when you look back on it all years later, you may still be confused.

From Tom Wheeler's "combat" situation he learned that choosing the environment in which one interviews a person can have a major impact on the quality of that interview.

Reporting in Third World countries is always difficult, both for foreign and domestic reporters. Leonard Sussman shares his experiences.

Reporting in Dallas on that Fateful Day

Jim Featherston

During my newspaper career, which spanned nearly twenty years, I occasionally felt like Joe Btfsplk, the old Al Capp gloom-and-doom cartoon character who walked around with a dark cloud over his head. I sometimes felt as if I were a jinx because I seemed to have been "there" when catastrophe or tragedy struck.

I was working for the Sunday *Vicksburg Post-Herald* on December 5, 1953, when a tornado devastated that historic and hilly Mississippi city. I shared a "local reporting under deadline pressure" Pulitzer Prize for the coverage of that disaster.

Then on November 22, 1963, I was nearby when President John F. Kennedy was assassinated in downtown Dallas. I helped cover that horrendous tragedy for the now-defunct *Dallas Times-Herald.* I also helped cover the trial of Jack Ruby, the man who killed the man accused of killing the president.

At the time of the assassination, I was covering the courthouse for the *Times-Herald,* and that is why I was nearby when President Kennedy was killed. The courthouse was near the end of the presidential motorcade route, and I had been assigned to call in information about crowd reaction in that area. I also was to catch some film thrown to me by photographer Bob Jackson who was riding in the motorcade.

I was not too excited about my assignment, which I considered minor, or the motorcade itself. At the time, I was forty years old, and the *Times-Herald* was the fourth newspaper for which I had worked since beginning my journalism career a dozen years earlier. In addition to the Vicksburg tornado, I had covered a number of big stories including the Emmett Till trial in the Mississippi delta and the Little Rock school integration crisis. I also had met a number of newsworthy figures, including John F. Kennedy

115

when he made a speech in Jackson, Mississippi, several years earlier when he was a U.S. senator.

At the time of the assassination, I was one of two reporters covering the courthouse for the *Times-Herald*, and we worked out of the courthouse pressroom along with a *Dallas Morning News* reporter and six newsmen from two Fort Worth-based television stations. The pressroom was straight out of Hecht and MacArthur's *The Front Page*, with dilapidated typewriters and odds and ends of camera equipment littering the tables along with overfilled ashtrays and empty beer cans. The atmosphere was downright unhealthy, but we loved it.

On the morning of the assassination, I arrived in the pressroom about seven o'clock, and, as usual, I was the first one there. Jerry Richmond, my *Times-Herald* cohort, came in a few minutes later muttering darkly about some anonymous "jerks" who had distributed anti-Kennedy handbills in downtown Dallas. Jerry had one of them in his hand. It was captioned "Wanted for Treason" and had two mug shots of Kennedy, one in profile and the other full face, just as if he were a criminal.

"This man is wanted for treasonous activities against the United States," the handbill declared. It then accused the president of encouraging race riots, betraying such friends as Cuba, upholding the Supreme Court in its "anti-Christian rulings," appointing "anti-Christians to federal offices," "turning the sovereignty of the U.S. over to the communist-controlled United Nations," and "invading a sovereign state with federal troops" (referring to troops sent to Mississippi when James Meridith became the first black student to enter Ole Miss). The handbill also accused the president of telling "fantastic lies" to the American people.

Jerry grumbled even more a few minutes later when he discovered our competitor, the *Morning News*, was running a full-page anti-Kennedy advertisement. This ad, bordered in black like a death notice, was sarcastically headlined "Welcome Mr. Kennedy to Dallas" and had been submitted by a self-styled right-wing "American Fact-Finding Committee." It accused the president of selling food to communist soldiers who were killing Americans in Vietnam. It also blamed him for the imprisonment, starvation, and persecution of "thousands of Cubans" and strongly hinted that Kennedy had reached a secret agreement with the U.S. Communist Party. "Why have you permitted your brother, Bobby, the Attorney General, to go soft on Communists, fellow travelers, and ultra-leftists in America while permitting him to persecute loyal Americans who criticize you and your administration?" the ad asked.

Later in the morning, Jerry and I and Jack Renfro, a television reporter, sneaked down the street for a beer. It was, after all, a festive occasion—at least that was our excuse for drinking before noon, but to be
truthful we used anything for an excuse back in those days. At any rate,
we talked about the presidential visit and unanimously agreed that nothing really bad would happen. Maybe a few anti-Kennedy signs or perhaps
a few boos, but nothing more than that, we agreed.

About the time we were drinking the beer, President Kennedy was being wildly cheered as he spoke to a large crowd in a parking lot outside
the Texas Hotel in Fort Worth, about thirty miles away. "Where's Jackie?"
someone yelled. Kennedy smiled, pointed to her eighth-floor window,
and replied, "Mrs. Kennedy is organizing herself. It takes her a little longer,
but, of course, she looks better than we do when she does it." The crowd
roared with appreciation. Later, Kennedy was warmly applauded at a
Chamber of Commerce breakfast, and when Jackie Kennedy appeared
later, she was greeted by about two thousand Texans, many of whom stood
on their chairs to cheer.

About 11 A.M., Jack Renfro headed for Love Field where the Kennedys
would be enthusiastically welcomed after their short flight from Fort
Worth. Jerry then left for the Trade Mart, where he was to be one of the
back-up reporters covering the President's scheduled speech. I went back
to the courthouse and talked to Jim Bowie, an assistant district attorney
and one of my favorite people. Jim also thought nothing really bad would
happen. Within a few months, Jim would help prosecute Jack Ruby for
killing Lee Harvey Oswald.

Shortly before noon, I went outside and took my place near the corner of Main and Houston streets to await the motorcade and Bob Jackson. The motorcade was to turn right from Main onto Houston, travel a
short block to Elm Street and zig-zag left toward the triple underpass.
The crowd had thinned out considerably in the Main and Houston vicin-
ity, and many of the spectators were people who worked or had business
at the courthouse. I was wearing a press card, which had been issued by
the police, on the lapel of my coat, and because of this a patrolman permitted me to step off the curb to await the motorcade. I noticed the skies
had cleared after a heavy overcast morning. It was as if the sun had come
out to welcome President Kennedy, I thought. It was a beautiful day, and
obviously no rain would fall on this parade. It was windy, however.

There was excitement as the motorcade approached, and I found myself getting caught up in it. When the presidential car approached, I rub-
bernecked toward Jackie Kennedy like everyone else. I had to restrain

myself from shrieking, "Hey Jackieeee!" like so many others along the motorcade route. I barely noticed President Kennedy or Texas Governor John Connally and his wife who were also in the presidential car.

Bob Jackson was in the photographers' pool car, which was seventh in the procession. As the photographers' car approached the corner, Jackson threw his film toward me. It was in a little paper sack, however, and a strong gust of wind caught it and blew it toward the other side of the street.

I ran through the motorcade to retrieve the film and then I heard the shots. I really did not recognize the shots as gunfire—I thought what I heard might be fireworks. However, I realized quickly from the reaction of the crowd something catastrophic had happened. One woman was hysterical.

I spotted a young lawyer named Frank Wright. "What happened?" I shouted.

"I don't know, but a woman down there was taking a picture of whatever happened," Wright replied, pointing to nearby Dealey Plaza.

I ran to Dealey Plaza a few yards away, and this is when I first learned the president had been shot. I found two young women, Mary Moorman and Jean Lollis Hill, near the curb on Dealey Plaza. Both had been within a few feet of the spot where Kennedy was shot, and Moorman had taken a Polaroid picture of Jackie Kennedy cradling the president's head in her arms. It was a poorly focused and snowy picture, but as far as I knew then, it was the only one in existence. I wanted it, and I also wanted the young women's eyewitness accounts of the shooting.

I told Moorman I wanted the picture for the *Times-Herald,* and she agreed. I then told both of them I would like them to come with me to the courthouse pressroom so I could get their stories and both agreed. When we got there, no one was in the pressroom except for a freelance cameraman doing some work for NBC. "What's up?" he asked. "The president has been shot," I replied. He laughed, thinking I was kidding. But when I got on the phone, and he realized I was serious, he ran from the room. The next time I saw him, several days later, he was still running.

I called the *Times-Herald* and told Tom LePere, an assistant city editor, that the president had been shot. "Really? Let me switch you to rewrite," he said, unruffled as if it were a routine story. I briefly told the rewrite person what had happened and then put Moorman and Hill on the phone so they could tell in their own words what they had seen. Moorman said she was so busy taking the picture that she did not see anything. Hill, however, gave a graphic account of seeing the president shot a few feet in front of her eyes.

Before long, the pressroom filled with other newsmen. Hill told her story over and over again for radio and television reporters. Each time she embellished it a bit until her version began to sound like Dodge City at high noon. She told of a man running up toward the now-infamous grassy knoll pursued by other men she perceived to be policemen. In the meantime, I had talked to other witnesses, and at one point I told Hill she should not be saying some of the things she was telling radio and television reporters. I was merely trying to save her later embarrassment, but she apparently attached intrigue to my warning.

As the afternoon wore on, a deputy sheriff found out I had two eyewitnesses in the pressroom, and he told me to ask them not to leave the courthouse until they could be questioned by law enforcement people. I relayed the information to Moorman and Hill.

All this time, I was wearing a lapel card identifying myself as a member of the press. It was also evident we were in a pressroom, and the room was so designated by a sign on the door. I am mentioning all this because a few months later Hill bad-mouthed me in a Warren Commission deposition taken by Arlen Specter (later a U.S. senator from Pennsylvania). She told Specter I had grabbed Moorman and her camera down on Dealey Plaza and wouldn't let Moorman go even though she was crying. She added that I "stole" the photograph. Hill said I forced them to come with me to a strange room and wouldn't let them leave. She also testified I had told her what she could and couldn't say. Her testimony defaming me is all in Volume XVI of the *Hearings Before the President's Commission on the Assassination of President Kennedy*—the Warren Report.

Why Hill said all this has never been clear to me. I later theorized she got swept up in the excitement of having the camera and lights on her and microphones shoved in her face. She was suffering a sort of star-is-born syndrome, I suppose.

It was a wild afternoon. While we were in the pressroom, Lee Harvey Oswald, the accused assassin, had left the Texas Schoolbook Depository where he worked as a stock clerk. He had aroused suspicion when he did not return to work after the assassination, and an improvised sniper's nest had been found on the sixth floor of the building. Oswald had first gotten on and off a bus before taking a taxicab to his rooming house in Oak Cliff, a section of Dallas west of the Trinity River.

Oswald's description had been broadcast to cruising patrol cars, and he was stopped by Officer J. D. Tippit while walking about a mile from his rooming house. When Tippit stepped out of his patrol car, Oswald killed him with four revolver shots. Oswald then ran into the Texas Theater about eight blocks away. He was spotted by the manager of a shoe store across the street who called police. The lights were turned on in the darkened theater, and Oswald was arrested after a scuffle during which he tried to shoot one of the policemen. "Well, it's all over now," Oswald shouted, then added: "I protest this police brutality."

Meanwhile, President Kennedy had been pronounced dead at Parkland Hospital about 1 P.M. About three hours later, at Love Field aboard Air Force One, Lyndon B. Johnson was sworn in as the 36th President of the United States.

That night I went to the Dallas police station where Oswald was occasionally hustled through the halls between interrogations. The hallways were crowded with dozens of reporters and photographers who jockeyed for position each time Oswald appeared. The atmosphere was sometimes chaotic. As I recall, two first-rate *Times-Herald* reporters, Jim Lehrer (later part of the MacNeil-Lehrer team on PBS) and Warren Bosworth (later an investigator for the district attorney's office) were covering that scene, and I left because there was nothing for me to do.

I ended up my long workday about midnight back at the courthouse pressroom, sharing a bottle of booze with Jim Koethe, a friend and a fellow *Times-Herald* reporter. Jim filled me in with information about Oswald that I didn't know. I also remember his telling me about the many coincidences of the Kennedy and Lincoln assassinations—that both men had vice presidents named Johnson and that Lincoln had a secretary named Kennedy and Kennedy had a secretary named Lincoln, and so on.

Koethe himself would die a violent death within a few months. He was found murdered in his apartment, and police theorize he was the victim of strangulation or a karate chop. The case was really never solved, and Jim's death has been linked to a conspiracy theory that contends an unusual number of persons (more than thirty) with direct or indirect connections with the Kennedy assassination died violent or unexpected deaths. The taxi driver, for instance, who drove Oswald to Oak Cliff was killed in a car accident, and one of Jack Ruby's striptease girls was murdered.

The next day was Saturday, and many people appeared at Dealey Plaza near the assassination site. Some were simply curiosity seekers, but many were genuinely grieved. Some brought flowers in tribute to the slain resident. I spent the entire day at the courthouse and around Dealey Plaza.

I interviewed Henry Wade, the state district attorney (and later of *Roe v. Wade* fame) who was another one of my favorite people. He said that oddly enough there was no federal law against killing the president, and that Oswald was to be tried in state court in Dallas unless there was a change of venue to another Texas city. He also indicated that Jackie Kennedy and Lyndon

Johnson, among others, probably would have to return to Dallas to testify at the trial. This all became academic when Oswald was killed by Jack Ruby. And now, of course, there is a federal law against killing a president.

Robert Oswald, Lee Harvey's brother, came by the district attorney's office at Wade's request, and I tried to interview him. The brother, who seemed like a nice guy, was a sales executive with the Acme Brick Company in nearby Denton. He pleasantly but no less firmly refused to answer my questions. Robert Oswald, by the way, kept his mouth shut for several years. He finally gave an interview to *Look* magazine, and later coauthored a book.

As the day wore on, a crowd began to collect on the Dealey Plaza side of Houston Street. The rear entrance to the county jail was across the street, and many were expecting Oswald to be transferred from the city jail that day. Undoubtedly, they were expecting to catch a glimpse of him. I remember my city editor, Ken Smart, calling me and asking me the size and mood of the crowd. I estimated the number and told him the crowd seemed more curious than angry.

I had expected to rest on Sunday. After sleeping late, I remained in bed watching television. It was my first opportunity to watch coverage of the assassination events. I was relaxed when about 11:30 A.M. NBC was showing the transfer of Oswald from the city jail.

Suddenly, a figure emerged from the crowd in the city jail basement and shot Oswald. There was a wild scuffling, and the gunman yelled: "You know me. I'm Jack Ruby!"

The NBC newsman on the scene, Tom Pettit, standing only a few feet away, hardly missed a beat. "He's been shot—Lee Oswald has been shot! There is panic and pandemonium," Pettit told the millions in his television audience.

I almost levitated from the bed in pure astonishment.

In the jail basement, Jack Beers, a *Dallas Morning News* photographer, triggered his camera as soon as Ruby leaped from the crowd with a gun. Beers got an excellent picture but Bob Johnson of the *Times-Herald* snapped his shutter a split second later and got an even better one. In Jackson's shot, Oswald is grimacing as the bullet tears into his body. Bob won a Pulitzer Prize for his photograph.

Minutes after Oswald was shot my telephone rang, and it was Ken Smart summoning me back to work. Among other things, I gathered information about Jack Ruby, whom I did not know but had seen around the *Times-Herald* building and the courthouse. Ruby, a nightclub owner, was one of those people who liked to hang around newspaper offices, radio stations, police stations, courthouses and other such places. The Dallas County sheriff, Bill Decker, knew Ruby well and told me about some of Ruby's relatively minor law violations. Ruby, for instance, had beaten up one of his striptease girls a few months earlier. That Sunday I also went to the subcourthouse in Oak Cliff to dig up some complaints filed against Ruby. The subcourthouse was closed on Sundays but was opened just for me.

In the days, weeks and months following that weekend, I wrote many stories dealing with the assassination and subsequent events. I remember writing the first story for the *Times-Herald* about the spontaneous out-pouring of money sent to the widow of Officer Tippit. She eventually received more than $640,000 as Americans opened their hearts and their pocketbooks to her and her family. I also interviewed Margueritte Oswald, the accused assassin's mother, among many others. I helped cover Jack Ruby's trial, and Jerry and I also covered many other legal hearings in-volving Ruby. We got to know Melvin Belli, the colorful, flamboyant San Francisco attorney who became Ruby's top lawyer.

Ruby was found guilty and sentenced to die in the electric chair, but the conviction was overturned by the Texas Supreme Court, which ruled that a change of venue should have been granted as requested by Belli. Ruby was in county jail in the courthouse for many months pending the appeal and then waiting for his second trial which was to have been held in Wichita Falls. During this time, I got to know his family, particularly his sister, Eva Grant, who frequently came into the pressroom while visiting her brother upstairs. I also got to know several of his friends. Ruby died of cancer while waiting for his retrial about three years after his convic-tion. I have never believed there was any connection between Oswald and Ruby as some conspiracy theorists insist.

I worked for the *Times-Herald* for another seven years, and I tried to keep up with all the various conspiracy theories and rumors, and over the past thirty years I have read and reviewed a number of books about the assassina-tion. Since joining the journalism faculty at Louisiana State University in 1970, I have spoken to many classes and other groups about the assassination.

Like millions of others, I have never been satisfied with the Warren Report conclusions. However, some people seem to think I should know what really happened because I was nearby when President Kennedy was shot. I do not. I am as mystified as everyone else.

Jim Featherston was a journalism professor at Louisiana State University for twenty-four years. In 1953, he won a Pulitzer Prize while working for the Sunday Post-Herald *in Vicksburg, Mississippi. He later worked as a reporter for the* Dallas Times-Herald. *When he retired from LSU in 1994, many of his former students raised money to endow a scholarship in his name at the school.*

Covering a Kind of Coup
in Buenos Aires

J. Laurence Day

I was putting the finishing touches on an overnight report that combined news from various bureaus in southern South America.
It was late in the evening. The Buenos Aires bureau of United Press International in those days had a large staff of Argentine reporters who covered
domestic news for capital, suburban, and provincial newspapers. There were
half a dozen Argentine reporters and four or five teletype operators in the
bureau that night. They were filing routine stuff. Theirs for the most part
were going to places like Mar del Plata, Mendoza, and Cordoba. Mine was
going north to New York, supposedly for distribution worldwide. But the
world wasn't much interested in soccer matches between Paraguay and Chile
or grapevine blight in eastern Mendoza province.

Actually, I was tending the store. All the good correspondents, all the
veterans, were over in Uruguay covering the Inter-American Economic
Conference. The nations of the hemisphere were meeting to discuss President Kennedy's Alliance for Progress.

Meanwhile, back at the UPI bureau on Belgrano Street in Buenos Aires,
I was preparing the overnight report—pasting together news reports that
had come in from other bureaus. I saw the Argentine journalists gathering around the radio on the domestic side of the newsroom. It was tuned
to a local station playing tangos. Piccollo, the fifty-five-year-old office boy,
brought a sheaf of teletype reports to my desk.

"Piccollo, what's going on? There's not a soccer match tonight."

"They've interrupted the program. There's going to be an announcement."

I grabbed my notebook and joined the crowd at the radio. As I approached, the reporters started taking notes. "...a profound revolution aimed
at freeing the country from its subordination to powerful economic interests. In our republic the revolution is desired by the people and the

123

fatherland emerges out of the wishes of the Argentine citizenry. Men of the armed forces with national sensibility and identified with the people are beginning the march toward our liberation...."

Was this the long-rumored coup to oust Argentina's first civilian president in years? Arturo Frondizi was elected in 1958 in the first election since the military overthrew dictator Juan Perón in 1955. Votes from the outlawed Perónista party gave Frondizi the presidency. He survived a serious coup attempt in 1959. He was accused of being soft on Perónism and communism. Troops massed around Buenos Aires, but at the last minute key military leaders remained loyal to the civilian government.

The last words of the rebel "manifesto" were followed by martial music. Rabinowitz, the chief of the local bureau, began barking orders, and the reporters scattered to their desks. The operators hustled back to their teletypes. Standing at one of the teletypes, Rabinowitz began dictating a lead for Argentine clients. Most of the morning newspapers were getting ready to close their early editions.

One of the reporters called to me from his desk. "You'd better get a flash off to New York," he said. In those days a flash was the designation for the most important, the most vital, news events. "Flash. Frondizi resigns." That was a flash. But what was this? I'd only been with UPI a few weeks. I was a "local hire." That's something that both AP and UPI said they didn't do, but did. I spoke Spanish well, had a degree in journalism, and daily newspaper experience. I had come to Buenos Aires on a scholarship. When my studies ended, and a Buenos Aires correspondent left UPI abruptly, I was hired.

I'd been at UPI long enough to have been burned. Soon after they put me in charge of the overnight report, I filed "urgent" press cables on a domestic airline crash. Our local desk reported that the plane had crashed into an orphanage on the outskirts of Buenos Aires. That's the lead I cabled to New York. In those days, "urgent" press cables took up to half an hour to reach New York. By the time the story got to UPI's Latin American desk in New York, I knew that the plane was down in a field several hundred yards from the orphanage. A bell on one of the teletypes started dinging. "Baires, your lead on plane hitting orphanage is exclusive, file followup soonest. When can you submit rescue art?" I knew what they wanted. They wanted pictures of firemen dashing through smoke and flames carrying little children in their arms. Luckily my boss, Dave Belnap, who was head of South American news for UPI, heard the radio report of the crash. He came straight to the office. With his skillful touch UPI was able to "row back" from the bogus lead, and cool the story down. After it was over, Dave briefed me on the finer points of news agency filing protocol, and told me to contact him before filing any more "urgent press" leads.

So when the "rebel proclamation" came over the air that night, I was cautious even though the newsroom was really jumping. The rebels came back on the air to urge the populace to support the revolution by gathering in Plaza Italia to demand Frondizi's resignation. Plaza Italia was a few blocks from the presidential residence in Olivos. The last words of the rebel communique were muddled by static. A reporter picked up the radio and began twisting the dials to get rid of the static. Suddenly the static stopped. The radio was silent except for a faint buzz. The reporter turned the dial to other stations. Nothing.

Across the way, Rabinowitz was standing behind one of the teletype operators, dictating a running story for provincial newspapers that were on deadline. A reporter shouted, "The radio went dead. We can't get any of the stations." Rabinowitz finished dictating a sentence, looked at his watch, and started dictating a flash.

"Flash... At 10:45 P.M. all radio stations in the federal capital went off the air."

Things were getting scarier and scarier. One of the local reporters was at my side insisting that I file a northbound flash. Instead, I picked up the telephone and dialed Dave Belnap's house. Dave was due back from Punta del Este to work on some transmission problems. As I dialed I voiced a silent appeal to the Great Gaucho in the Sky that Dave made it back to Buenos Aires.

I said a quiet thanks when Dave answered the phone. I summarized the situation.

"Have you filed anything northbound?" he asked.

"No I haven't."

"Good. Don't file anything. I just turned on my radio and it's playing music. This doesn't smell right. The *ambiente* isn't right for a *golpe* (coup). It's the wrong time of the year. Hold everything till I get there."

Just then bells on the international teletype from New York—the Chester wire—began dinging like crazy.

URGENT "Sao Paulo (UPI) local radio stations report that a military coup is underway in Argentina. They attribute the information to ham radio broadcasts from Buenos Aires. URGENT Bogota (UPI) Radio Splendid reports that rebel troops have taken over several Bueno Aires radio stations and that a military takeover is underway. URGENT: BAIRNES BUREAU Bairnes, urgentest. Unreceived Baires file on coup. How?

Santiago, Chile (UPI) An offical in the foreign ministry said that Chilean troops on the border with Argentina may be put on alert after reports of a coup attempt in Argentina."

I walked over and told Rabinowitz that Dave Belnap's radio was working fine. Rabinowitz picked up the office radio and gave it a shake. It suddenly came back to life.

"*Eso es un lio de la gran puta* (This is trouble from the great whore.),*" yelled Rabinowitz as he dashed to the teletypes to dictate a rowback on the flash that had reported Buenos Aires radio stations off the air.

Piccollo yelled across the room that a long distance call was coming in. I ran over and grabbed the phone. I could hear the operator talking with someone. Then Bill Horsey came on the line. Bill joined UPI in the 1920s or 30s, and was now dean of wire service correspondents. He was day editor in Buenos Aires. Horsey was in Punta del Este covering the Alliance for Progress.

Just then Dave Belnap burst through the door, crossed the newsroom, and picked up the dispatches from the Chester file. He scanned them quickly, then dictated a message to the teletype operator sending it at the priority cable rate.

"08112303 New York, offknock filing exBogota, exSantiago, other sites. We on top situation here. Belnap."

Horsey was yelling into the phone, asking what we going on. I panicked. I dropped the phone and crossed the room.

"Dave, Horsey's on the phone from Punta del Este."

"Fill him in and tell him not to file anything from Punta del Este."

Dave grabbed a phone and started dialing. I went back to the desk where the receiver was dangling on its cord and said, "Horsey, Horsey?" The line was dead. I learned later that Horsey was one of dozens of correspondents using one outbound phone line and that he had only two minutes to talk. He had hung on until another correspondent jerked the phone out of his hands.

Dave called me over. "The rebels have taken over a radio station and a telephone exchange across town. Call a remise and get over to..."

I wrote down the address and called the chauffeur service. No one, not even Belnap, had a car in Buenos Aires in those days. There was no such thing a drive-it-yourself car rentals. UPI hired a company that provided cars and drivers at a moment's notice. I didn't wait for the elevator. I dashed down the four flights and ran out on the sidewalk. A big black 1952 DeSoto swung around the corner, drove up the block and double parked. Then I realized I had left my reporter's notebook upstairs with my coat.

"*Momentito,*" I yelled to the driver.

I ran back up the four flights, dashed into the newsroom, grabbed my coat, a second notebook and some pencils and ran back down the stairs.

I leaned forward and gave the driver the address. I didn't know anything about that part of town. The center of Buenos Aires is beautifully laid out, but outside the center, beyond the city planned by nineteenth century French architects, is urban sprawl that only a few cities in the world can match.

As the driver wove the car skillfully through late night theater traffic on Calle Cordoba, everything seemed normal. Florida Street had the usual number of strollers and window shoppers. After we passed Nueve de Julio, the world's widest street, and Plaza de Congresso, I began running out of landmarks. The driver started winding in and out of narrow, darkened streets. Then he stopped the car at a dark, cramped intersection.

"*Aqui estamos, senor,*" said the driver.

We were at the corner of Tweedle Dee and Tweedle Dum, as far as I was concerned. I was lost. The driver pointed down Tweedle Dee Street.

"The telephone exchange should be down there about a block and a half. I'll wait here with the car," he said.

There were no street lights, and the sky was overcast. Buildings on both sides of the street were dark, their windows shuttered. The driver might as well have been pointing to the mouth of a cave and saying, "You'll find the bear in there, sir."

I made my way through the darkness, feeling my way down the middle of the street with the tips of my toes. It sticks in my mind that the street was cobblestoned, but I won't swear to that. I covered a block and reached the next cross street. It was even narrower and darker than the one back where the driver lounged against the fender of his DeSoto, smoking a cigarette.

I moved into the second block, inching my way. Half a block down a "colectivo" was sitting crosswise in the street. Buenos Aires has thousands of these small independently operated buses; this one had been commandeered by the rebels.

("How did you get to the coup attempt, Daddy?" "I took a colectivo.")

The front end of the bus was sitting on one sidewalk, and the back end was on the sidewalk across the street. The back end of the bus was jammed against the building, but it looked like there was room for me to get around the front end of the bus. I had inched my way around the hood of the bus when I heard two sounds at the same time. Behind me was the sound of footsteps. In front and above me came a voice giving a curt command, "No se mueve." But I did move. I took another step because the meaning of the command had failed to register. "*No se mueve,*" said the voice again.

As I took one more small step, a third curt command came simultaneously with the unmistakable sound of an automatic weapon being prepared to fire. At the same time, a voice behind me hissed in Spanish, "*Che,* don't move, he'll kill you."

I froze. My head was tilted upward and I could see, finally, the dim outline of a man crouched in a window ledge five feet above me. The barrel of his machine gun was trained on my belly button.

I found my voice, and fortunately Spanish came out of my mouth.

"I'm a correspondent. I'm from UPI. I'm just trying to find out what's happening."

Behind me the voice that had hissed, spoke up, "I'm from *La Prensa*, don't shoot." The guard, with a lot less curtness, called out for his superior officer. An officer—don't ask me what rank—came out of the door, down the steps and stood in front of me. The reporter from *La Prensa* slid around the front of the bus and stood beside me. The officer told us to scram. We scrammed. The *La Prensa* reporter said he was on his way to the radio station that had been taken over. I joined him for a short ride; he had a car and driver, too. By the time we got there the rebels had surrendered and troops were moving out. I located a pay phone in a bar and called Belnap. I told him about the incident with the bus and reported that the radio station had been captured. He said he had that information. The rebels still held the telephone exchange where I had been. It had been reported that the rebels were cadets from a military school under orders from a "Commander Maldonado." The *La Prensa* reporter was headed back that way. I hitched a ride with him and we spent the rest of the night on watch. The military moved in some heavy machine guns and a couple of mortars, as I recall. They kept giving the rebels ultimatums: "You will surrender by...or we'll blow your house down." Each time the deadline passed, and the rebels didn't come out with their hands up, the military set another deadline. Finally about six in the morning the rebels surrendered. I called Belnap, but he already had it. In the growing daylight, the area looked more familiar. Belnap told me to head back to the office. I walked a couple of blocks and spotted a subway entrance. I went downstairs, inserted my token, and rode back to Plaza Mayo. I was writing a wrapup when a phone rang near my desk. The reporter who answered it looked over at me and said, "He's here. He's right here. He just came in."

Then he raised his hands in the universal gesture of the mystified, and hung up the phone.

"That was your driver. He kept calling in all night long and we kept telling him you're still on the story. How did you get back here?"

"I took the subway," I said.

J. Laurence Day is a journalism professor at the University of West Florida. He has worked as a foreign correspondent for UPI and a copy editor for the Minneapolis Tribune. *A two-time winner of senior U.S. Fulbright awards, Day has concentrated his research on international communications, directing workshops for professional journalists in fifteen Latin American and Caribbean countries and Sudan.*

So What's Your First Question?

Tom Wheeler

I had conducted interviews under less than ideal conditions, but nothing prepared me for my encounter with rock guitarist Ted Nugent. He was known for two things: his ability to play louder and faster than any of the hapless chumps who came up onstage to challenge him, and also his image as a rampaging hunter gnawing the bones of a fresh kill. I interviewed him for *Guitar Player* in the late 1970s, at the mammoth Cal Jam concert in Los Angeles. Although his entrance onstage before 100,000 rabid fans would prove remarkable for its bombast, it was no less impressive than his earlier entrance into the restricted backstage patio. Resplendent in fringed buckskin and coon tails, he strode across the Astroturf like a warlord, taking big steps that left his entourage scrambling to keep up.

About fourteen of us crammed into one end of a trailer. Ronnie Montrose and his crew were at the other end, and he was warming up for his own performance by playing electric guitar at earsplitting volume just on the other side of a flimsy partition. Among the four photographers in our group was Lynn Goldsmith, something of a minor celebrity in her own right; when the other shooters weren't taking pictures of Nugent, they were taking pictures of her. A stunning Asian-American model perched on Nugent's lap, primping and pouting as the shutters clicked. Security guards in muscle shirts barked into walkie-talkies while assorted hangers-on guzzled free Budweiser, oblivious to the fact that some journalist was about to attempt a rational interview for publication—a cover story, no less.

So Ronnie Montrose is blasting away practically in the same room, a gaggle of freeloaders is gabbling like geese, unseen voices are crackling over walkie-talkies, flashbulbs are popping all over the place, a

129

rock concert is raging outside, and Terrible Ted, one hand on the long leg of his trophy date, turns to me and grins like a pirate and hollers over the din, "So what's your first question?"

That conversation (if you can call it that) yielded all of about three inches of usable copy. But fortunately I had also taped conversations before and after the official appointment—over squid at Benihana's, in a thirty-minute limo ride, at the soundcheck, over the phone. With no audience to regale, Nugent was downright articulate. I got my cover story.

Tom Wheeler is the author of The Guitar Book *and* American Guitars *both Harper & Row) and the former editor of* Guitar Player *magazine. He is an associate professor at the School of Journalism and Communication at the University of Oregon, where in 1993 he won the Marshall Award for innovative teaching.*

Reading Between the Lines

Leonard R. Sussman

American journalists working abroad often rely on local reporters for leads and background. Most countries, particularly the forty-five developing nations I have visited, present special problems for the American correspondents.

Whether stationed in a developing country or parachuting for a brief reportorial visit, the foreign journalist meets not only different cultural, ethnic, and linguistic backgrounds, but starkly different journalistic ground rules. Generally set by authoritarian governments, these rules influence foreign correspondents even if—sometimes but not always—they are relatively free to secure information and report it.

The visiting reporter is often alerted by local newspaper accounts to a story that should be covered for publication abroad. The pressures which distort local coverage must be understood, however. I sat with the editor of a black newspaper in South Africa during the height of apartheid's fierce racial separatism and oppression. He had been a Neiman Fellow at Harvard, and was a fine editor in a fiercely controversial post. As he edited that day's news, he had a lawyer at his side full-time to weigh every word destined for publication. The editor had already served time in prison for breaching one of a hundred government restrictions on local journalism. Not long after I left the country, the editor died at an early age of a heart attack. The strain of editorial judgments in the face of oppression had taken its toll.

Not all governmental restrictions end that morbidly. Shortly before South Vietnam was overrun by the communist North, I spent a week discussing press freedom with journalists in the South. They faced a recent decree that increased restrictions on their reporting. I learned from them at least as much as I taught. They had an intricately developed code for

131

reporting forbidden facts in a way their readers understood. American journalists covering that country learned the code by reading the local press. For example, a short story appeared one day stating simply that a young girl in a southern town had died from eating cactus. Readers immediately learned from this story that serious food shortages—information forbidden to journalists by censors—had hit that town. Why else would a child eat cactus?

In many countries where censorship prevails, reading between the lines, as this coding has come to be known, is a vital necessity for the visiting journalist, as well as for local journalists and their public.

One of the finest journalists I met in black Africa was the editor-in-chief of a national wire service. While his country was overrun by a dictator, he worked abroad for several years at the Associated Press. When the dictator left, the editor returned to head his national agency. It was impoverished. I stood beside him one day as the sole functioning teleprinter received news from abroad. The machine was so ancient it printed only figures, no letters. A young staffer converted the figures back into words. Yet this editor performed professionally even as the political tide, again, turned grim. American journalists who passed through this country learned to estimate the quality of the man and his output against the growing oppression. To protect him, visiting correspondents would attribute information to other sources—not the usual form taught in journalism schools.

This did not save him, however. He was thrown out of his post, his life threatened. When I last heard from him, he was driving a truck. But even that did not save him. He was quietly advised to flee the country. He did, but then learned that his family was threatened. He returned home to a grimly uncertain future.

American journalists who value their own freedom often undervalue the courage and determination of many third world journalists who labor each day under subtle and not-so-subtle threats to their lives and careers. I still recall a letter Ellie Abel showed me. When he was dean of Columbia University's Graduate School of Journalism he received a message from an African student. Abel said the student was "extraordinarily good," and had gone home in a rather triumphant glow to take charge of a rather important news organization in his own country.

Two years later Abel received this letter stating, "You taught us all too well…. This, as you know, is a one-party system and the things I've learned in America have made it difficult—probably impossible—for me to function in such a system….The system lays upon us an affirmative obligation to praise the regime and above all to glorify the head man. The dilemma of adhering to professional ethics and at the same time trying to satisfy the whims of politicians is a headache."

That letter, Abel concluded, was written from outside the country. The man had given up journalism, as well as his country, to prepare himself for a new career in another field, another place.

Since 1990, there have been many changes in governments in Asia, Europe and Africa. Journalism is somewhat freer on all three continents. But the absence of market economies to support competing news media still permits considerable governmental pressure on local journalists and influences international reporting. It requires visiting journalists to employ greater sophistication in interviewing sources who today use "democracy" and "free market" to mask still-subtle controls over information and reporting.

Leonard R. Sussman teaches journalism at New York University and is a senior scholar in International Communications of Freedom House, an agency devoted to strengthening free institutions around the world. He is the author of Power, the Press and the Technologies of Freedom: The Coming Age of ISDN *and* The Culture of Freedom: The Small World of Fulbright Scholars.

chapter **nine**

Covering Death

Covering death is a paradoxical experience for reporters. Certainly no one wants people to die, yet a slow news night can be extremely boring. When a reporter gets word of a murder or fatal accident, he or she is energized. It's time to do what one is trained for, and the drama involved can be exhilarating—so much so that is is easy to forget one is dealing with real people, people whose lives have suddenly, violently, ended, and with relatives who must deal with that loss.

I once rode in a patrol car with a police officer for a day-in-the-life type feature story. It was a fairly routine day, which I was afraid was going to make a rather dull story. Then he got a call on his police radio that neighbors had not seen an elderly woman for days and were afraid she might be dead in her house. We both perked up. As we raced to the house, we wondered what we would find. A murder, maybe? The dull day had just gotten livelier.

As it turned out, the woman was not dead; she had just gone away and failed to inform her neighbors. As the officer and I continued our ride, we both confessed to a certain thrill when we got the call. We realized that reporters and police officers are both trained for action, and that we like it. We didn't want anyone to be hurt, but at the same time a routine day isn't very interesting—or very newsworthy.

Since most reporters do want to cover the big story when it happens, it's easy to understand Michael Shapiro's rush to be The First Reporter At The Scene. It's also easy to understand his feelings of ambiguity as he looks back on the experience.

Michael Sewell's reaction to a chance to ride in a medevac helicopter in Vietnam was similar, and one any inquisitive reporter would have—great story. It was only when he sat beside the dying Vietnamese woman that he realized the pain behind the story.

One of the most difficult parts of covering death, as Joann Lee discovered, is calling a grieving relative. But as hard as her task was, she learned much more about her subject from the girl's family than from a police blotter. I also once had to talk to parents of a murdered girl. At first I protested because it seemed so intrusive, but my editor made a good point—if we are going to write about someone we ought to give family members the opportunity to comment. They quite often have something they want to say.

James Bow and Richard Smyser also had to cover death, and in doing so learned an important lesson. In these kinds of situations, the standard journalism rules don't always apply. In covering tragedy, it's best to go with your instincts.

Wanting to Be There

Michael Shapiro

In 1979, on the Friday of Memorial Day weekend, an American Airlines DC-10 took off from O'Hare Airport, rolled on its side and slammed into the ground, killing all those aboard. I was then twenty-six and working in the basement office of the *Chicago Tribune*'s suburban *Trib* in Des Plaines, a short drive from the crash site. I was quite full of myself. I was not, to put it charitably, the most well-liked person in the newsroom, having transported to the Midwest the aggressiveness that was tolerated in my native New York, but seldom appreciated by my colleagues in suburban Chicago.

But I could not help myself when it came to seizing, though never stealing, stories. And so it was, on that Friday afternoon, less than a year since my arrival, that word came of the crash. A group of us hurried outside and saw the plume of black smoke and recognized that we sat very close to the story of the day.

That was a rare sensation indeed, in a newsroom where the comprehensive coverage of the city council and pithy profile of the village manager were regarded as the kinds of journalistic pursuits that would endear us to our employers. Now a great many people lay dead in a field not five minutes from our office, and our editor, a pleasant-enough fellow who later went on to be a highly successful ad salesman, walked ponderously to the big map on the wall, there to determine into whose beat the plane had crashed.

Now you are reading this thinking, "Into whose beat? Are you mad? Get the staff out there!" But that was not how things worked in our newsroom. Everyone had beats, and beats were the backbone of our newsgathering enterprise. The man lacked a feel for the moment.

But he was in charge. And in that capacity he looked carefully at the map and determined after much calculation that the plane had crashed

136

into an unincorporated section of a local town. No one covered unincorporated sections. We covered towns. He turned from the map and searched out the eyes of the woman who covered the nearest town. Sad to say, she was already looking away, having been a half step ahead of him and sensing the inevitable.

She did not want to go. She did not say this, but it was clear as she rose from her chair that this was not work that pleased her.

And who could blame her, except for, of course, a journalist? I looked at her, standing frozen at her desk, and was mystified by her reluctance to sprint from the room, out to her car and to the crash site, there to be The First Reporter At The Scene.

The editor informed her of her task as if he was reading a long and undeserved prison sentence. I watched as she headed for the door, longing to be in her place.

From time to time in the years since, I have thought of that moment and of my reaction then, and in the moments that followed when I raced up to the editor's desk, dropped to my knees, placed my hands together in supplication and begged him to send me, too. I have thought of my eagerness to go and of the complete absence of any thought about how that which I so much wanted to witness was a place of quick and awful death. I did not think of the dead. I thought only of the story and, of course, of myself getting it and writing it.

Which is just what I did. My begging succeeded. The editor, having no idea what to do with a story of this magnitude, relented and let me, and later others, go. I sped to the scene, getting as close as I could before pulling into a restaurant parking lot. I flagged a volunteer fireman and offered him $20 to take me to the crash site. He turned on his red light and siren and raced between cars. When we got to the site he asked for his money, but I brushed him off and ran past the police lines, flashing my press pass.

The woman who had preceded me by twenty minutes arrived half an hour later. I told her the story was mine. She did not protest. Others soon followed, but the piece, I made clear, would be mine to write.

The *Tribune* did not want our story. It did not want our reporting or anything else we'd gathered. We were the "little Trib" and they would send the big boys and girls from downtown. Never mind that they got there an hour later.

So we concentrated on the people who came to gaze, the onlookers drawn to the horror. We watched the people straining at the police lines, trying to catch glimpses of body parts, the crowds that gathered on the surrounding bluffs, and the many others who streamed to the field, there to place themselves in close proximity to an event of great importance.

We were not, of course, writing about ourselves. We were journalists, which meant that gaping was our work. We did not just come to look. We came to observe and distill and record for all the rest to read. We stayed for a very long time that afternoon. Only later, at dinner, did I notice that my suede shoes were tinged black with the soot of the crash fires.

I can still look at the story I wrote and, in that rare moment in reviewing past work, not wince in horror. It was not a bad piece. The detail was vivid and the story moved along and brought the scene alive nicely.

But I should not be saying this. I should speak of a certain degree of revulsion with myself and my eagerness to be there, as close as I could get, looking and recording and thinking of my lead.

The night of the crash, a group of us went out to dinner and one friend turned to me, or rather turned on me, criticizing the ghoulishness of the enterprise and of all those who wished to take part in it. I told her that she, as a reporter, should know better, that such stories were what we raced to write for a living and that if she could not stand it perhaps she was in the wrong line of work.

My comment was as uncalled for as hers was misguided. There are journalists, wonderful journalists, who avoid the world's horrors. But there is something inside journalists that makes them want to be there, at the scene, at the moment; it is a quality that those who are not journalists cannot understand.

It does not make us bad. It is just who we are. We do not think about what we are about to see. Sometimes we do not think much at all before we go. We leap and look and later drink and tell bad jokes as a way of avoiding the kinds of painful reflections that might stop us from leaping again.

Once I had a student who could write well and was eager to succeed. By chance she happened to interview a man whose daughter had been murdered in what was a celebrated crime in New York. It was clear from her telling of the story that the man wanted her to ask him about his daughter and her death and her recently convicted killer.

"What did you do?" I asked, and she replied that she changed the subject and left.

"How could you?" I asked, and she said that she anticipated that his story would be too upsetting to hear.

I told this story to a group of friends, all but one journalists, and their reactions, save for the non-journalist's, were the same. They were best summed up by the most senior member of the group, a legendary foreign correspondent who said, simply, "Tell her to go to law school."

The rest of us nodded and laughed, except for the nonjournalist, who thought we were an absolutely awful lot. Nothing we could say could convince her we were not. I believe that we stopped trying and opened another bottle of wine.

Michael Shapiro is the author of three nonfiction books. His work appears in such publications as The New Yorker *and* The New York Times Magazine. *He is an assistant professor at the Columbia University Graduate School of Journalism.*

Death and the Lessons of Life

Michael Sewell

"**T**oday, I grow up or I die." There was more than a passing story behind that thought about death and life's "lesson plans."

The day was September 18, 1967. It was a typical day for that place and that circumstance in my young life. Working as a daily newspaper reporter, I was in Danang, South Vietnam, as a correspondent. Later, from the vantage of experience and distance, I would realize that it wasn't just inexperience that caused the problem that day. It was a combination of naïveté and my occasional fascination with danger. The normalcy of my family and of when and where I was raised contributed to my naïve nature. Who knows what led to my sometimes reckless interfacing with danger? It manifested itself with automobiles first; I liked to drive fast. Very fast. Then it showed up in high school football when, at 134 pounds, I discovered that I liked to take on 200, 220, or 240-pound linemen and backs while playing defensive end. Perhaps that was really naïveté, or just stupidity. At any rate, that kind of thinking got me to the 363rd squadron, Marine Aircraft Group near China Beach that day. In a green, hot squad hut, I was doing that for which I was educated and employed—interviewing people. These people happened to be involved in a nasty little war halfway around the globe.

At 1 P.M., I was sitting in the office of Capt. J. B. Barr, 25, U.S. Marine Corps. On his desk were copies of *Stars and Stripes, Playboy,* and an old copy of *The State,* the Columbia, South Carolina, newspaper for which I wrote. We chatted alternately about the war and our alma mater, the University of South Carolina. Barr had graduated a year before me, but we had not known each other at the campus of over ten thousand. The conversation was more than a bond between alumni, for in Vietnam men looked for any bond of friendship, any chance to forget the danger or how far away from home they found themselves. They looked mostly to the day they would return to "the world," and all of them could tell you exactly how many days it would be—plus a wake-up.

Barr handed me a Canada Dry ginger ale, the best thing to come my way since orange juice and real eggs earlier that morning in the officer's mess on the *U.S.S. Oriskany*, out in the Gulf of Tonkin. The topic returned to the war; my task was to find out how the war was going for men from South and North Carolina, the circulation area of my newspaper. "I must be the luckiest pilot in the war," said Barr. "I've flown a medevac (medical evacuation mission) every day in the year I've been here. Only been on R & R for three days. I've never been shot down, and, so far as I know, never been shot at." That sounded amazing to me, but I assumed he was telling the truth. Why would he lie about such? But the naïveté in me didn't consider the possiblity that all of that luck could change abruptly. Within minutes, as we continued to talk, Barr received a call for a medevac. "I've got to fly south of here, toward Chu Lai. Ground fire has been very light lately. Do you want to go along?" "Sure," I answered. Was it the naïveté or my subconscious desire for a little danger that caused the confident, blurted reply? Maybe he had just done an excellent job of salesmanship (Barr was a business administration major at the university) with his "luckiest pilot" label.

We walked to his VH-34 Delta helicopter. The appellation, "Animule," was painted on the fuselage. My eyes scanned the entire aircraft. No bullet holes. "Have you ever flown in a helicopter?" asked Barr. My response was "No," and he explained that the feeling when a helicopter ascends or descends rapidly was similar to being in a falling elevator. This was a problem I could handle. I had landed and launched from an aircraft carrier only hours earlier. I had flown in a C-130 transport in a thunderstorm. I had flown civil air transport and China Air Lines, and even Piedmont back in South Carolina. No problem.

Barr introduced me to the crew chief, a thirty-five-year-old veteran from Kentucky, and his waist gunner, a seventeen-year-old who looked rather apprehensively at his M-60 machine gun. I would learn later, post-naïveté, this is one of the most dangerous jobs in the war. Barr went to pilot the chopper, and shortly the rotors began churning into the most memorable and recognizable sound of the Vietnam war: whoomp-whoomp, whoomp-whoomp. "Where's the corpsman?" I asked. "Oh, we've lost over half the medics in this squadron," replied the crew chief, "so there's not a corpsman available." My naïveté began to dissipate. "Something is not quite consistent here with the conversation Barr and I were having in the hut," I thought.

"Pick up those grenades off the floor," the Kentuckian barked at the waist gunner. "Any stray shots hitting one of those and our asses will be blown out of the air." Barr, the luckiest pilot in the war, began to look farther away to me than just in the cockpit. "Here," said the crew chief, proffering body armor to me, "you might want to wear this chest protector. Personally, I think it's better to sit on it, 'cause you're more likely to get hit in the butt in a helicopter." By now, I was much less relaxed and much more serious about attempting to assess this situation. Before I could ask anything, the crew chief picked up a grease gun (a light machine gun). "You know how to use one of these?" He handed it to me. "I don't think you'll need it ... but you never know. I've been shot down twice. The last time there were VC everywhere ... but then our choppers got us out." His voice trailed away, muffled by the whoomp-whoomp. I was psychologically stunned. "Mama," I thought, "what is your favorite son doing here?" I was seriously thinking about cancelling my participation in this venture when the helicopter lifted off. "Too late to change your mind now, dummy," I thought.

Perhaps the Kentuckian recognized that look on my face, the look on the faces of most men going into combat for the first time. I glanced at the young waist gunner and saw it on his face. He couldn't have done this much, I thought, for he had told me as we prepared for liftoff that he had been in Vietnam only two weeks. "Jeez, he looks more scared than me," I thought. It did not reassure me. Later I would recognize that look on other faces in Vietnam and know—really know—the feeling in the pit of the stomach that goes with it. In a tone he no doubt meant to be reassuring, the crew chief said, "You know, you can't really hit anything more than fifty feet away with those damn things," pointing to the grease gun he had given me. "I'd just as lief have a pistol," he said in his deep hillbilly twang. "Oh, great," I thought. "Now I've gone from fellow alumnus telling me he's the luckiest pilot aloft to a suddenly, unfortunately enlightened journalist listening to the grim teachings of a battle-hardened veteran. Why didn't I get this lucid vision of the several distinct, but definitely negative, other possibilities connected with this mission before we left?"

"What the hell will I do if we're shot down?" I thought. "The possibility of being shot down—not to mention probability—is bad enough, but I'm not a soldier and I'm not trained in any fashion to deal with such a circumstance." I tried to use humor to lessen my anxiety. "I'll shoot anything that moves. People, in any kind of uniform or clothes, water buffaloes, chickens, palm trees, the moon. Woe to anything near me if we go down. My God, what if I run out of ammunition? What if the rescuers won't come near me because I'm shooting every creature on earth? Stop, stop." I forced myself to stop the imaginary what-ifs. This wouldn't help. "Spilt milk is spilt milk," I thought. "I must remain calm and do my job. Okay, I'm a journalist. Take pictures." So, I began doing my job, shooting pictures with my 35mm Pentax through the bay door. One last philosophical thought was permitted: A rather naïve twenty-four-year-old had climbed into that Delta bay fifteen minutes earlier. He would get out, God willing, a little wiser and a little older. "Today, I grow up or I die," I thought, considering two of the possibilities of that flight. The former, of course, was far more to be preferred, but I didn't realize then what lay ahead that would make it a profound and emotional possibility, not simply the most desirable.

Within a few minutes we reached our first stop. A yellow flare near a large, white building with a tin roof marked our landing zone. The two gunners became particulary alert and seemingly apprehensive. I copied their behavior. Suddenly, in a swirl of dust, three soldiers raced to the chopper with a man on a blanket. They dumped him, literally, in the bay and ran full speed back to the building. The man was an ARVN (Army of the Republic of Vietnam) soldier who had malaria. We immediately lifted off and sped for a hospital. I surmised that the Delta crew was worried about more than saving fuel, but, absent a head-set, I didn't know what kind of information was being passed along.

After dropping the ARVN at a hospital, we flew to a hamlet near Bong Son. There six women—three old women and three young girls—were loaded into the Delta. There were only two stretchers, so the other four lay on blood-soaked straw mats. All had lost limbs, an arm or a leg, hand or foot blown away or mangled by a mine or booby trap. "No corpsman," I thought. "This is just terrific." The women were conscious. One looked at me with pleading eyes and said something in Vietnamese. I didn't understand, couldn't understand. I wanted to hurl away my camera; I felt like an intruder. Worse, I felt so helpless because I wasn't trained to give medical assistance. The woman who had spoken held out her hand, her fingers closing and opening, then closing again, just as a child might reach for candy. That feeling came back into the pit of my stomach, but it wasn't fear or anxiety like any experienced before. I was looking at Old Man Death. He wasn't stalking me, but I couldn't do anything to help keep him from his quarry. The crew chief did what little he could. He repeatedly came over to the woman next to me, speaking to her by nearly burying his face in hers; I couldn't hear what he was saying, nor even tell if he were speaking Vietnamese. The wind blew a bamboo mat over the face of another woman near me. I pulled it away and secured it. A young girl, about twenty years old, flopped a leg on the old woman immediately adjacent. I gingerly moved the leg back. My attempts to help weren't much, and they certainly weren't enough. Five minutes from the hospital, the old Vietnamese woman next to me died. The crew chief looked at me, his veteran face pained and said, "There was nothing anybody could do. She lost too much blood." Death was not completely foreign to me; I had been present when my father died the previous year. A lot of the anguish came back. I hated death, even though I recognized its inevitability for all of us. This was an unnecessary death. I doubted that this child-like old woman understood terms like democracy or communism or the war that killed her. Like me, she just wanted to live. She died with only a foreign soldier to comfort her last moments. I was her other witness. At that moment, I didn't want to be a journalist. I didn't want to be there. This was not the way to grow up, I thought. I didn't eat for over twenty-four hours.

Later, back in Saigon, I thought about the Kentuckian and his companion. They had to live with this all the time. They had to fear the bullet and, perhaps worse, the daily agony of torn and suffering and dying bodies. I could go home and leave it behind; they had to wait for the final wake-up—or the medevac, or the body bag. Now, when I think about the "day that I grew up," I still see that tiny opening-and-closing hand and those pleading eyes and remember the helplessness. I remember how I began to realize that my own safety was dependent upon other people. I realized that the chopper pilot's greatest luck may have been that he was in the cockpit, not in the bay. And I realized that life and death's greatest lessons were learned by the Vietnam veterans, not the journalists, certainly not the politicians. I can now fully understand the veteran who said, "We didn't have a childhood. All we had was Vietnam." My flirtation with danger and my emotional involvement with death was brief. But what about the year that seventeen-year-old Marine waist gunner "grew up"?

Michael Sewell is the chairman of and a professor in the department of mass communication at Texas Wesleyan University. He was a reporter for The State *and has taught at the University of South Carolina-Spartanburg, the University of Alabama, and Texas Christian University.*

How Do You Feel About That?

Joann Lee

Just about every semester without fail a student will bring up the "How do you feel?" question.

It usually begins with a discussion on ethics, and the lines reporters eventually learn to draw for themselves. A student will raise the issue of why reporters have to do certain things, such as going up to someone who has just lost a friend or family member to ask, "How do you feel?"

There is no good answer for why reporters have to ask certain questions. Only that if we shut ourselves off to asking the most difficult questions, sometimes the most powerful moments of a story can go untold.

Of the thousands of television news stories I have covered, one in particular has remained etched in my mind over the years. It will be nineteen years since I reported on it, and it is still a story I carry with me. It is a tragic story with no happy ending.

I had just started working as a reporter for a Sacramento television station. I was on the night shift, working with a camera woman who also had been hired recently, so we were both relatively new at our jobs.

The word came in from the sheriff's office late one afternoon. A young woman had been reported missing. Her car was found at a local shopping mall with the keys still in the ignition, a hamburger half eaten in the front passenger's seat. The last time anyone heard from her, she had called home saying she needed to have someone pick her up. She said she would wait in her car. When her father arrived, he found the car, but his daughter was gone.

We interviewed the officer in charge, and then went to the area where the car was parked to get some video. Within a few hours we learned that her body had been discovered, dumped in a barrel a few miles out of town. There was water in her lungs.

145

My news director told me to get more information about the victim and to interview her family. I was not expecting this. It was a terrible tragedy, and in my mind the facts had already been provided by law- enforcement officials. Why disturb people in their hour of grief? Neither I nor my camera woman felt comfortable with the idea of charging in on the family.

Without telling my boss, "No, I won't do it," I made myself a deal. I would knock on the door, introduce myself, and if I was told to go away, I would, and just tell my boss the family didn't want to talk.

We pulled up to a well-manicured lawn with a white frame house just as dusk was coming on. As I walked up the stairs I still remember telling my camera woman to stand by, but not to shoot anything.

A minister opened the door. I identified myself, apologized for intruding, then asked if it was possible to speak to a member of the family. I said I was there to find out more about the young woman who was killed. He told me he was her uncle, and invited me in.

As I entered the living room, a picture of a young woman with a dazzling smile stared at me from atop the grand piano. It was her high school graduation picture. I asked if it was possible to get a copy of the picture for my story. I still remember how quiet it was in that room, even with all the people inside. There were about twenty aunts, uncles, friends, and siblings, as well as her parents. They began to talk.

"She would have started college in three weeks," one person told me.

"She liked to play tennis, and she sang in the church choir," another said.

"She played the piano," someone added.

Others sat in the room trying to remember when they last saw her. And so the pieces began to take shape. Little by little the victim was no longer a statistic whose story was read off of a police report. She was an eighteen-year-old girl, with dreams and aspirations, someone who was loved very much by her family, a family now too stunned, angry, and hurt to talk about the crime. A family who, in a sense, wanted to talk about her life in positive terms, so that as her name was broadcast over the news that evening, she would not be portrayed only as a victim of a brutal crime, but as a person with a life, a family, a future.

This is my "How do you feel?" story.

I never asked the question that night. I saw the answer in their eyes, heard it in their voices. My camera woman did shoot the victim's graduation picture. We also got a shot of her family, as they sat around the living room. Her uncle talked on camera about her plans and hopes.

To this day I repeat the story to my students. I think the young woman would be close to forty now, if she were alive. The sheriff's office caught two male suspects within three days of the murder. They reportedly had offered her a lift.

The "How do you feel?" question is direct and blunt. But the intent is not to be brutally insensitive. Other words can and should be found to arrive at the purpose for asking that question, for the answer derived goes to the heart of one of the reasons for journalism: to render meaning when often times events seem senseless. It is not always possible to do this, but sometimes the opportunity is there. I know reporting on the story about a murdered young woman will never bring her back. But who she was, and how she met her murderers—while eating a hamburger in her car and waiting for a ride from home—are reminders that unforeseen things can happen to anyone. By telling her story in just that way, perhaps people will become more aware of how life can turn on a dime, at the wrong place, at the wrong time. That she was young, planning to attend college, and came from a loving family, adds to the commonality of the experience, and thereby the story becomes even more powerful.

There are those who would argue that my presence in the home, and speaking to her family, was not essential. Maybe not, but it gave me as the reporter a sharper sense of who the victim was, and that helped me write about her. Even though the brutal nature of her death dragged her identity into the local media spotlight, it was nonetheless important that she be remembered for more than the crime committed against her.

The "How do you feel?" question does not happen only in broadcast. It cuts across all kinds of journalism. Reporters ask it every day, in different ways, whether they are doing magazine profiles or a breaking newspaper story. Good reporters will find ways of getting the answer without seeming insensitive. Being a responsible journalist means knowing how to get answers, especially to the tough questions.

Joann Lee is an assistant professor and codirector of journalism studies at Queens College in New York City. She has worked as a television news reporter in Sacramento, Chicago, Philadelphia, and New York City. She has taught journalism for the past eleven years, seven of those as an assistant professor at Columbia University's Graduate School of Journalism.

RFK's Shooting

James Bow

For anyone who witnessed the shooting, or its imme-
diate aftermath, of Robert F. Kennedy in a Los Angeles hotel kitchen, the
memories are more complicated than those expressed in media
retrospectives. They evoke personal thoughts, trivial as well as profound.

As one of several Associated Press staffers who worked on the story, I
arrived at the scene shortly after Kennedy was shot. Somehow, the facts I
reported turned out to be coherent. The private memory that remains in
my mind is more tangled.

Three scenes remain the most vivid to me. One involves a cab driver,
another, the disheveled lobby of the sprawling Ambassador Hotel, and
the third, an interview with what looked like a gravely injured man.

Another AP reporter and I took a cab toward the Ambassador from
our downtown news bureau, where we both had been writing stories on
that day's California primary election.

Television sets in the AP bureau had carried coverage of Kennedy's
victory speech in the state's Democratic primary, followed by on-screen
confusion and shouts about a shooting off-screen. Within seconds, two of
us had been assigned to head for the Kennedy election-night headquarters at the Ambassador, a few miles from our office.

We ran for a cab and, heading west on Wilshire Boulevard, saw an
ambulance speeding toward us. We followed it, suspecting it carried
a victim from whatever had happened at the hotel. The other reporter
left the cab when the ambulance stopped at Central Emergency Hospital.

I asked the driver to hurry on to the Ambassador. In our ambulance
chase, we had already told the cab driver about the story we were investigating. Some explanation was needed after we had ordered a fast U-turn
on a major street.

The young, bearded driver's reactions to the words "shooting" and "Kennedy" were similar to what many other Americans would experience when they got the news. He swore. He was angry, then grief-stricken. But he kept driving. Later he tried to refuse money for the fare: I tried to force him to take it. I think the $10 bill landed on the pavement.

At the hotel, a reporter who had been covering the Kennedy victory had already left to report what he had seen. Since I had no chance to talk to him, I didn't know who was shot, or if one or more gunmen were still roaming the hotel. My job was to get a coherent account from authorities and witnesses of what had happened to piece together with reports from the hospital and police headquarters.

In the hotel lobby, clumps of people talked or cried. At that point, chairs, tables, and lamps from the lobby furnishings had been dumped in the large fountain in the center of the room. My interest was in talking to people about what happened in the Kennedy party, not about furniture. I never found out whether the furniture hurling was part of a panicked scramble to get out of the lobby or an almost automatic reaction by supporters to the initial word that another Kennedy had been shot.

The lobby was too far from the shooting scene to find any eyewitnesses. I headed outside and back toward the kitchen exit, and saw people being carried out on stretchers. I soon learned that the gravely wounded Kennedy already had been taken to the hospital, very likely in the ambulance we had followed; others had been shot as well.

One man on a stretcher, wearing a Kennedy campaign straw hat, seemed alert. The hat was lopsided on his head covering a shadow of blood on the stretcher. He was Paul Schrade, head of the United Auto Workers in California. Either he was not in severe pain, or he was hiding it, for he was able to fill me in on what he saw in the few minutes before he was lifted into an ambulance.

I later learned Schrade's head wound was not severe. That was a relief. He had given me the outline of what happened, a beginning.

Later, other sources helped to fill in the sequence of events. By that time, I was in the Embassy Room. I saw ex-football player Roosevelt Grier, one of Kennedy's supporters, sitting alone at a table. If a three-hundred-pound man could look crumpled, he did.

I started over to talk to him, then stopped. I can't say why I interviewed an injured man and didn't speak to a healthy ex-football star, except that Grier seemed injured also, perhaps more deeply.

James Bow has taught at Central Michigan University and the Ohio State University School of Journalism.

Covering Sensitive Stories Accurately

Richard D. Smyser

In the matter of accuracy, I tell my students, we are all conceived in sin. Then I hold up a poster showing a big, shiny red apple with an arrow dead center in it and, underneath, in big red letters, Joseph Pulitzer's famed dictum: "Accuracy! Accuracy!! Accuracy!!!"

In the 1970s Levi Strauss & Co. sent out these 2- by 3-1/2-inch stickers with the Pulitzer admonition in bright red letters too. Reporters could stick them on their telephones or typewriters. I still have one and pass it around for students to see.

Why was Levi Strauss so concerned about accuracy? Why might Xerox, Coke, or Band-Aid have mailed out similar stickers?

By now someone in the class has caught on. All jeans aren't Levis, so if reporters mention Levis in news copy, the L should be capitalized and the writer should be sure he or she is referring to the genuine article with its registered trademark name.

Accuracy! Accuracy!! Accuracy!!! I'm consciously evangelical. Once a student called me an "accuracy freak," and I couldn't have been more pleased.

You just can't be too careful, I preach. Check, recheck, and recheck again. Remember also that there's no substitute for direct contact with your news sources. The more go-betweens, the greater the chances that the information will be fuzzy and incomplete.

I ask the students to remember the children's game (some call it "gossip," others "telephone")—the one where someone whispers something to someone else and they whisper it to someone else, and then to someone else, and how distorted the original becomes.

Accuracy is crucial in all stories, but, I admonish, it's especially crucial in reporting personal tragedies. To assure the most accurate, the most sensitive story, you must get as close as possible to the people directly involved; yes, that means the spouse of the plane crash victim, the parents of the child killed when a car struck the bicycle.

But isn't this intrusion on grief, the students ask anxiously? Not if the approach is made with consideration. Not if the tragedy-struck spouse or parents know that your purpose is accuracy, I say. Then I tell two stories.

Two bright, talented high school seniors—a boy and a girl—were killed when their car was struck broadside by a very drunk driver late one Friday night. The next morning, at their editor's insistence, reporters called the victims' homes and asked if they could come to talk with someone there to be sure they had complete information, and especially complete personal information about the deceased teenagers. In both cases the parents agreed to see the reporters and, when they met with them, not only did they offer information willingly, but pictures too—their favorite pictures.

The account of the accident appeared at some length—lots of detail on the collision itself, much information about the young victims' interests and activities and the favorite pictures. The next day, immediately following both funerals, both sets of parents came to the newspaper office. Seeing them walk into the newsroom, the editor (me) froze. What had we done so wrong that would prompt them to come in person at a time like this?

We hadn't done anything wrong. The parents just wanted to tell us how much they appreciated our story. It was, they said, full and accurate, and they thanked us for contacting them directly.

Several years later, there was another fatal accident. A mother and her two small children had driven to the Knoxville airport, about forty miles away to meet the plane on which her husband, and the children's father, was returning from Chicago where he had received a scientific award. They had planned a family dinner out on the way home.

At the airport, the woman was told that the plane would be an hour late. It was suppertime, and the children were hungry, so she drove to a nearby fast-food place to get them a snack. On the short drive back to the airport, a car crossed the median strip and hit them head on at high speed—another drunk driver. The mother and both children were killed. One can only try to conjure the agony of the father when his plane arrived and he learned why his family was not there to meet him.

It happened on a weekend, so there was time for the news staff to gather detail. Again, direct contact was made with the home of the victims, and the surviving husband, by then surrounded by grieving relatives and friends, was willing, even anxious, to talk with a reporter.

The next morning, just as the reporter was finishing writing the story, the husband, accompanied by two friends, appeared in the newsroom and asked to see the editor. Could he please, he asked me, read what had been written?

It was, of course, well-established policy that copy was not available to sources for review. Further, I wondered as I fumbled for an answer, what if he wanted us to leave out some essential part of the story? What if he wanted us to include something that, for news purposes, we would feel very inappropriate?

What could, should, I do?

I made a quick and much more emotional than rational decision. I just could not, under these circumstances, refuse this distraught man's request.

So I seated him at the computer terminal. He was computer literate and followed easily my instructions on how to call up the story.

He sat there for maybe ten minutes scanning the story up and then back down the screen. He read. He reread.

Then he rose, turned and looked at me directly and said softly, "It is all right. Thank you." Then, with one of his accompanying friends on either side, he walked from the newsroom.

His wife and children were gone. He wanted to be certain that the newspaper account of the deaths was correct.

Accuracy! Accuracy!! Accuracy!!!

Richard D. Smyser has taught at the University of Tennessee; the University of Alaska, Anchorage; the University of Nebraska, Lincoln; and Pennsylvania State University. He has worked for the Chester (PA) Times *and the* Oak Ridger, *and has been active in national newspaper organizations.*

Ethics

At some point all journalists have to make decisions in reporting or writing that go beyond the basic whos, whats, wheres, whens, and hows. Since the answers aren't always clear-cut, the choices they make end up reflecting their own personal ethics.

Bob Russell still regrets the decision he made when he covered up his reporting mistake rather than take responsibility. P. J. Corso, on the other hand, thinks she made the right ethical decision, even though it cost her a great shot.

Two other contributors, Jim Pratt and Mike Ludlum, had to decide what to do about a story which could get worse *because* of their reporting. Pratt's coverage of a fraud didn't put the fraud out of business, instead, it gave him publicity and increased his sales. On top of that, Pratt had to decide how to handle a bribe. Ludlum, for his part, learned that reporters shouldn't get too caught up in the story of the moment and lose perspective on what else is happening. And they have to decide for themselves where to draw the line between being a good reporter and a good human being.

That line isn't always easy to draw, as Sandra Dickson found out. She had to find a way to protect her sources and also maintain her journalistic independence and credibility in the face of threats by Cuban government officials. Should she bow to censorship and turn over her tapes to save her sources, or should she fight to get her powerful story out? She thinks she made the right choice.

Robin Andersen presents us with another journalistic dilemma. We as journalists make it a point to present both sides of a story in an effort to achieve balanced coverage. But Andersen makes us question this rule by showing how "balancing" a story can distort the news more than it clarifies it.

And, finally, Maurine Beasley reminds us all of why we spend so much time trying to get it right and trying to make the proper decision. What we report really does matter.

153

An Act of
Sheer Moral Cowardice

Robert H. Russell

In the summer of 1968, I was a twenty-four-year-old reporter at United Press International's one-person Maine statehouse bureau in Augusta, where the lawmakers were debating whether to impose Maine's first-ever income tax, the most controversial issue to come along there in years.

The Senate leadership kept the legislature in session beyond its traditional June 30 adjournment date to deal with the issue, but they were having trouble getting a quorum; some lawmakers, sensing a no-win vote, were laying low. So the leadership sent the state police out to round up enough recalcitrant members to hold a vote.

It was a sweltering day in early July; lawmakers were milling around for hours waiting for a quorum call, and we reporters were wandering around, interviewing people for background material. I picked up a rumor floating around the capital that one of the senators (I'll call him Smith) had been located by the state police but had refused to accompany them to the statehouse. I made a mental note to check it out, but in the hectic hours to follow I never got around to it.

Finally the quorum bell sounded, the vote was held and the bill passed. Since the House had previously approved it, and the governor's signature was a foregone conclusion, we had our big story: Maine would have an income tax. Reporters rushed to file, and I started to bang out my story over my teletype. As I piled on the details, the scribbled note about Senator Smith slipped into the story as confirmed fact, and I flew out of the office to get a belated start on my holiday weekend.

On Monday morning, Senator Smith came to my office, accompanied by a state police official, and they assured me the police had not located Smith on Saturday and that my information was false. Smith said angry constituents had upbraided him at church on Sunday for ducking the vote. Smith was not angry with me and settled for my promise to run a retraction over the wire.

Now even then UPI was financially shaky and perpetually fearful of libel suits. If I sent out the retraction, my bosses in Boston would learn of my reporting lapse, which exposed them to a potential suit, and perhaps fire me. Fearful of losing my job, I sent out a vaguely worded item quoting Senator Smith as "denying reports" that he had refused to attend the senate session, but remaining silent as to the source of the original story.

I never heard another word from Smith, so my job (and perhaps career) was safe, but I have always regretted what I did. I tell my classes with a sheepishness that has faded only slightly over the years that failing to verify the rumor, which may have damaged Smith's career, was unforgivable, but that refusing to take responsibility for my story was even worse, an act of sheer moral cowardice.

Robert H. Russell is an assistant professor of journalism at Indiana University of Pennsylvania and formerly was an instructor at Marietta College in Ohio. He has worked for the Detroit Free Press, UPI, *the* Evansville Press, *and the* Greenburg, PA, *Sunday* Tribune-Review. *He is the coauthor of* Behind the Lines: Case Studies in Investigative Reporting.

A Journalist's Camera
Never Lies

P. J. Corso

I walked along the city street dressed down—baggy pants, faded windbreaker, dirty tennis shoes, backpack—but soon realized my clothes didn't hide the loaded camera I pointed at a corner known for drug dealing. My Minolta SRT201 might as well have been a Colt 45. No sooner did I raise it to my eye when I felt a tap on my shoulder.

"You're a cop, aren't you," a woman snapped. I quickly unzipped my backpack, pulled out my student I.D. and explained I was just getting an exterior shot of the residential hotel for my photography class. With the scowl of a barroom bouncer, she matched my face with the mug on my I.D. Her expression didn't change as she handed back my card and walked away.

When I photographed that hotel nearly ten years ago, I thought the only way to take a photo was to approach your subject, say who you are, what you want and ask for permission. But I know a few things now that I didn't know then. As a journalism instructor, I know the vernacular. What I did is called reporter as intruder—I emphasize the word intruder because I remember the fear I experienced when invading someone's territory with a camera and how my presence changed the status quo. I also know the options. It's easy to avoid a photo subject by shooting from a distance with a telephoto lens.

Since that encounter, I've worked as a freelancer and staffer for various publications and learned how to function in a system of deadlines, story quotas, and now-or-never opportunities. I became adept at taking what I needed from interviewees and racing back to the office. Rarely did I give in return—not even a promise to send a copy of the article when someone asked.

Now that I've given up full-time journalism for teaching, I ask my students, "Is it ethical for journalists to conceal their identity in order to get to unaltered truth? Isn't that what a tape recorder and a telephoto lens are for? Or is this an invasion of privacy and deception?" These questions had become academic for me until recently.

En route to a city university, I routinely pass a block near the bus terminal where homeless people have settled. I expect to see cardboard boxes and buggies and shopping bags, but one day I spotted something that moved me to take out my camera. Between the sidewalk and a wire fence was an old reading chair with a circular indentation at the top center of the pillow where I imagined someone routinely rested his or her head over the years when the eyes got heavy. Beside it, the settler had put an end table with a plant positioned exactly in the center. In front of the chair, a pair of men's shoes were neatly arranged.

A few "doors" down was another pair of shoes, men's loafers hanging on two slats of a picket fence like two capped teeth. The settler had put the fence along the front of his cardboard box, leaving a foot or two in between—enough room, I imagined, for a row of tulips. Seeing this man's loafers cupped on those two slats reminded me of a trip I took West where I saw ranchers cover their fences with old cowboy and cowgirl boots.

When I saw those pairs of shoes and thought about the homeless men who walk the streets in them every day, I realized they were a part of Americana that most of us never see but should. Deciding to photograph the shoes was the easy part. The difficult decision was how. I found myself asking the same ethical questions about reporters concealing their indentity that I pose to my students.

I got off the bus, took out my camera across the street from the settlement and was tempted to shoot because the men didn't appear to be there. And if they were, I knew flashing a faculty I.D. wouldn't bail me out this time. I raised my camera and paused—I didn't want to exploit them. It would be like photographing someone's living room or yard while they were out. I put the camera down and wondered how I'd reciprocate if I did decide to come back and get their permission.

I figured I could offer these men prints. Of course the ideal would be to teach them to take the photos themselves, but I realize, having worked with homeless men before, that like any population, they all aren't inclined to be creative. I once planned to get residents of a Pittsburgh shelter to write sketches for a play, but it turned out they preferred to do the talking and I do the writing.

I aimed my camera again, but I couldn't stop thinking about Charles, one of the homeless men I interviewed who wanted very much to participate in the play's production. He read initial drafts, came to rehearsals, and befriended the actor playing his character as well as myself and the other writer. I put the camera away and decided to wait until the men were there. I'd return with my gear later that week.

In those few days, the homeless settlement was destroyed. Cardboard boxes were flattened. Buggies were wheeled off, and the remaining contents of shopping bags spilled onto the sidewalk. The reading chair and picket fence were gone. And needless to say, the men who filled those two pairs of shoes were gone too. City officials had apparently shooed everyone away.

I regret that I didn't have the chance to meet them, but I'm not disappointed for myself. Now I realize their sense of urgency was far more pressing than mine. I lost a photo-op. They lost their homes.

When I discuss reporting approaches with journalism students, I share this experience and we discuss the trade-off. Because I chose to be an unobstrusive reporter, I ended up with no photos, which obviously would have put me in a bind had I been on deadline. Instead, I left with a deeper sense of respect for these men and the mental photographs I can take out each time I pass this block. I see one man resting his head on the chair with a newspaper on his lap and the other leaning proudly on his picket fence. I'd like to believe that a journalist's camera never lies.

P. J. Corso has taught journalism at Hunter College of the City University of New York and the New School for Social Research. Her articles have appeared in the Christian Science Monitor, USA Today Magazine, Philadelphia Inquirer, *and* Editor & Publisher.

How to Handle a Charlatan— and a Bribe

Jim Pratt

What do you do when a charlatan claims your investigative report didn't put him out of business, but increased the sale of his "Miracle Cure"? He stuffs money in your shirt pocket and races out the door saying, "Take your reporter to dinner and have a steak on me."

Pulling the bill out of my pocket I tried to give it back, but he was gone. It's still a felony to take payola in broadcasting. What I thought was a late 1960's ten dollar bill had one more zero on it. One hundred dollars, good money now, a lot of money in 1969. What was I to do?

Even worse, why would our in-depth report that debunked a "cure all" medical device promote an increase in its sales? Our ombudsman "Hot Line" reporter, Roger Davis, had received complaints about the ionized board and set about to investigate. He found that the board was manufactured for plants and not for human use. It cost a little over $19 in a gardening catalogue, but was being sold for just under $200 by the charlatan as a cure-all for asthma, arthritis, heart palpatations, back pain. The list went on. The newspaper ad claimed the charlatan could do "back flips after sleeping one night on the board." When asked in an interview if he could do back flips before he slept on the board, he said, "Oh yeah! I used to be an acrobat in the circus."

The report contained indictments from the American Lung Association, the Arthritis Foundation and the American Heart Association. The Federal Trade Commission had filed a complaint over the faulty advertising. It was a thorough, factual report that left no question that the board was worthless as a cure. Yet the report increased sales.

Selective perception had to be involved. People in pain, and so desperate for help, heard only those things they wanted to hear about the cure and disregarded the fact that the board cured nothing. The message had to be repeated somehow to attempt to erode those beliefs, always with the hazard we might sell more boards.

The one hundred dollar bill had been folded into an airplane while I thought. Another thought flashed through my mind, "I could sure use the money. Nobody knows I have it ... except the receptionist. That S.O.B. is getting rich off sick people, and this money came from some poor person looking for help." I flew my plane across the newsroom.

The next flight was in the manager's office. My plane made a three-point landing on Jim McCormick's desk. McCormick picked it up, saw what it was, and pushed it in his shirt pocket.

"You'll throw it back when I tell you where it came from," I said. And he did. The television station manager did not have any more ideas on what to do with the money than I did.

Roger came in, and I flew my plane in his direction and told him the story. He suggested we give the money to one of the groups trying to put an end to the ionized board as a wonder cure. "And we can give the money in the charlatan's name," I said. "It's next to giving him back the money, and it may do some good."

We set up a camera in the newsroom and told this story as we gave representatives of The American Lung Association and The American Heart Association fifty dollars each in the name of the charlatan. It gave us another opportunity to reinforce the uselessness of the miracle board.

The charlatan disappeared, the ads were gone from our area and we heard no more about sales and hundred dollar bills. It sure made us wonder about the effects of television reporting on our audience. The best we can do is report as fairly and accurately as possible. Our audience will only reinforce what they believe and disregard the rest unless the message continues and, over a period of time, crumbles some of those predispositions.

This occurred at KVII-TV, Amarillo, Texas, in my tenure as news director (1968-75). The story has been told many times to my Radio News Writing classes at Ole Miss. It is one of a myriad of "war stories" I've used. I told my classes, "I can give you the roadmap to good reporting and writing. And can show you the dangerous curves, potholes, and steep grades, but you still have to drive it yourself to know. You have to build your own experience and if you survive, you'll be a journalist."

Jim Pratt is an associate professor emeritus at the University of Mississippi. He has been a consultant in West Africa, training radio news and information producers for three radio stations in rural Liberia, and a news director at several TV stations in Texas.

Don't Get Too Caught Up
in One Story

Mike Ludlum

Many people consider Boston to be one of the nicest, most livable cities in the United States. It's sometimes called "the San Francisco of the East." But there was a time, not so long ago, when things turned ugly in Boston.

Everyone knew trouble was coming, but no one was sure just how bad it would be. Newspaper, magazine, television, and radio reporters from all over the world were dispatched to Boston to chronicle the upcoming events. The time was September, 1974. The city was about to deal with a problem that other cities and towns around the country would face right through the end of this century: how to end de facto racial segregation in the public school system. Federal courts were demanding that action be taken. In Boston (other cities would face similar rulings) a federal judge had determined that busing would be the most effective remedy. Thousands of students would be bused out of their own neighborhoods to schools in other sections of the city. The white parents of many of these students vowed it would never happen. They were fully prepared to flout the federal court. They would do whatever it took to protect their way of life, which they saw as seriously threatened. They would fight to preserve their neighborhood school system. The parents were backed up by many elected officials at the state and local level, including some very vocal members of the Boston school board who helped to fan the flames of dissent. Emotions were running high. The potential for serious violence was obvious—and frightening.

A few days before the opening of school, Senator Edward Kennedy showed up at a rally in front of city hall where thousands of people had gathered to protest the desegregation order. They came from mostly Irish, solid Democratic neighborhoods where the Senator and the Kennedy

161

family are generally respected. He had come to urge calm, but they were in no mood to listen, and they turned on him. They shouted insults and threw tomatoes and eggs. They unplugged his microphone so he couldn't be heard. They seemed to grow angrier by the minute, and some began chasing him. One woman yelled, "You ought to be shot, Senator. You ought to be shot." He hurried to the safety of a federal office building where dozens of people outside pounded on a window with their fists. One of the panes shattered, the pieces crashing to the floor. The demonstrators cheered. It was a harbinger of things to come.

During this period, I was the news director of WEEI, Boston's only all-news radio station, which was owned by CBS. I had a staff of excellent reporters who would be spending very long days and nights covering the developments that were about to unfold. All of us in the newsroom—reporters, anchors, editors, and news writers—knew we would be sorely tested. We would be dealing with many unpredictable and potentially explosive situations. We knew we could contribute to the tensions if we didn't play it right.

The mayor's office was concerned that the media could add to the problems, especially since so many reporters came from out of town and from other countries and weren't very knowledgeable about Boston. On the Sunday before the scheduled first day of school, the mayor asked all members of the media to attend a special briefing. City officials would be there to answer their questions and do whatever they could to minimize the expected confusion. At that meeting the Boston bureau chief of the Associated Press advised all out-of-town members of the media to keep their radios tuned to WEEI because we were expected to provide thorough and timely coverage.

Thursday—opening day. The buses rolled, the protestors were out in force and the police were prepared for trouble. The center of the anti-busing sentiment was white, Irish-Catholic South Boston. Black children were being bused in, and white youths and, in many cases, adults were ready with stones and rocks to hurl at those hated yellow buses. In the early days, many black parents were afraid to send their children into "enemy territory" so they kept them home. On the third day of the school year, *The New York Times* reported that "chanting bands of white youths roamed the streets of South Boston protesting court-ordered integration. Throughout the morning, policemen mounted on horses and motorcycles blocked and cut through groups of young whites trying to stage protest marches, while helmeted squads of the tactical force, wearing blue coveralls and combat boots, sealed off the corners."

There were twenty-two arrests that day. In one instance, two black youngsters were arrested for stoning a bus carrying white students in the

Dorchester section of the city. In another incident, five people were hurt when a public transit bus with a black driver was trapped on a street and stoned.

Day after day, the troubles continued and our reporters stayed on the job. While we worked, we learned a lot. We quickly realized that constant reporting on marches and stonings and other instances of violence must be balanced by other events going on in Boston. It's easy to get caught up in the story of the moment and lose perspective; the press is often guilty of doing just that. But we determined to balance our coverage by reporting on educational innovations being tried in some of Boston's schools. Even though 20,000 school children were being bused, 74,000 were not. So Boston's public education system was not total turmoil. A fair amount of real education was going on, and we made special efforts to talk about that.

During these months, my office got lots of calls from blacks and whites—parents, students, and educators who wanted to comment on our coverage. I personally took as many of these calls as I could because it gave me a good perspective on what people were feeling and thinking. We got some good constructive criticism from representatives of all sides of the controversy and some good ideas on angles we were missing.

One evening I called our reporting staff to a meeting. The idea was to have a free-for-all discussion of our coverage. What were we doing right, where could we improve, were we being as responsible as we could possibly be? With all that we were seeing and experiencing (including threats to our personal safety) were we still keeping our personal biases in check and being straightforward and fair in our reporting? One reporter (we'll call him Dave) raised a question that got everyone talking. If a reporter sees a person in danger of being seriously harmed by another person, should the reporter intervene to protect the threatened individual? Such an occasion had, in fact, arisen. Dave argued forcefully that the reporter should not intervene because, in so doing, he would be taking sides, or at least be perceived to be taking sides, and the credibility of his future reporting on the subject would be damaged. Another reporter immediately took issue, saying a reporter should not stand by and describe an assault when he could be of aid to the victim. Other reporters at the meeting weighed in with their views, which varied in intensity and content. All in all, it was a fascinating discussion, and worthwhile because the reporters had been so busy with the story, they barely had time to sit back and think about some of the broader issues.

As for my opinion: I disagreed with Dave. I think it's better to be a human being first and a reporter second.

Mike Ludlum, an associate journalism professor at New York University, has been a broadcast journalist for more than thirty years, including more than twenty years at CBS in jobs ranging from newswriter to executive producer and news director. In radio, he helped establish the successful all-news format at WCBS in New York and later at CBS-owned WEEI in Boston. In television, he was an associate producer at WCBS-TV in New York and later was head writer for Good Morning America.

Campaign for Cuba

Sandra H. Dickson

Sumptuous tropical fruits, a crisp white tablecloth, a soft warm breeze.

It was time to relax and breathe easier. Over our small cups of strong Cuban coffee, we could talk about the footage we still needed to shoot, the officials we still needed to talk with. Our stay in Cuba was almost over. We'd gotten some great video for our documentary on U.S.-Cuban relations, and we'd managed to interview six Cuban dissidents, many of whom had only recently spoken out against human rights abuses in Cuba.

When we arrived in Cuba in July 1991, we had no idea we would be able to talk to any of these artists, poets, and intellectuals who had decided that they could no longer remain silent about conditions in their country. Their public criticism of Castro and the Cuban government or what they called their "Declaration of Democracy," had cost them. Some had lost their jobs, been harassed by pro-government mobs and attacked in the official Cuban press. (Later, several would be imprisoned.) We weren't quite sure how to find these people. Cuba's phones rarely work, not to mention that there are few phone books (only ones with the names of people who had died fifteen years earlier) and, if the dissidents had phones, they would likely be tapped. But we were lucky. A Cuban we had met and talked to the day before arranged for us to meet the dissidents. He proposed that we rent several taxis and pick up the dissidents at various spots around Havana and then travel to a house about 15 miles outside the city. And so we did. The interviews went well. The dissidents were outspoken in their criticisms of Castro and the Cuban government and eloquent in their pleas for greater freedom.

Back at the hotel restaurant, it was time to relax and relish our success. Or so I thought. Looking up from my first sip of coffee, I saw an official

165

from the foreign ministry standing in the doorway of the restaurant. He was clearly agitated. He asked me and the executive producer to step outside the restaurant. He said he had something extremely urgent to tell us—clearly it was not going to be a recommendation on what dessert to order. He began by saying we were in big trouble because we had broken Cuban law by interviewing a Cuban dissident who had been granted conditional liberty (a sort of house arrest) and that we had misled Cuban officials as to the purpose of our documentary. In his words, it was obvious that we wanted to distort the true picture of Cuba by focusing too much on malcontents and counterrevolutionaries. Ministry of interior officials (state security) wanted our tapes. If we refused, they would take them anyway and we would be expelled from Cuba. We, of course, refused. We had an obligation to our sources. They certainly didn't expect us to turn over their interviews to the Cuban government. Besides, we all knew the importance of journalists being independent and credible—and certainly our credibility would not be enhanced if we willingly turned over our tapes to Cuban officials. This was the beginning of a lengthy debate between us and Cuban government officials and between Cuba's foreign ministry office and state security, all of which occurred while we were confined to our hotel. Foreign ministry officials argued that we should be allowed to keep the tapes, that American journalism demanded an examination of the negative as well as the positive. State security, on the other hand, felt that we, like so many American journalists before us, were trying to portray Cuba in the worst fashion possible.

For the remainder of the evening and the next day, we were held under house arrest. However, we were not bored during our confinement. We argued strenuously with Cuban officials, while they argued strenuously with each other. We were betting that the Cubans would not expel us because of the upcoming Pan-Am Games; that is, they wouldn't want a potentially embarrassing incident just before the games.

With each refusal on our part, they would huddle and come back with a new counterproposal:

- Proposal #1: Give us all your videotapes, including ones that do not contain the dissident interviews. If you don't, we will arrest the dissidents. Our Response: No. (We knew that they didn't need our tapes in order to arrest the dissidents. After all, this was a country which had been chastised by several international human rights organizations for repressing free speech and civil liberties.)

- Proposal #2: Give us the tapes with the dissident interviews and you keep the rest. Response: No.

- Proposal #3: Give us the tapes with dissident interviews, we will review them and give them back to you in a few hours. Response: No.

- Proposal #4: Let a Cuban official watch the tapes in your presence or, in other words, the tapes will not leave your possession. Response: No.

After Proposal #4, the Cuban officials lost patience. We were told that state security was on its way to search our rooms and take the tapes. We waited anxiously. I straightened my room a little—didn't want them to think I was an untidy person. A tense hour passed, then another. They never came that evening. In the morning, we walked down to the lobby and several large fellows (trying to look inconspicuous) followed us as we walked the length of lobby and out to the patio by the pool. Finally, the Cuban official who had been serving as our contact arrived. He told us, much to our relief, that state security had decided to let us keep our tapes; however, we would not be allowed to do any more shooting for the duration of our stay. But this was not the end of the world. We were leaving the next morning.

The final morning of our ten-day visit was a gorgeous Caribbean day—not a cloud in the sky, the Bay of Cuba glistened like diamonds. We loaded several taxis with all our equipment and made our way to the airport, still concerned that state security officials might change their minds and confiscate our tapes before we left. But our departure went without a hitch. We boarded the plane, tucked the tapes under our seats and leaned back to enjoy the beautiful flight from Havana to Miami.

The thirty-five-minute flight didn't give me much time to reflect, but it was long enough to think about how far we'd come since we began this documentary. Five faculty and five students had worked for more than a year shooting and conducting interviews in Washington and Miami, researching and reporting the complexities of U.S.-Cuba relations. More than twelve months of preparation had culminated in this trip to Cuba. But as I was engaging in this pleasant reverie, basking in the warm sun streaming through the plane window, I did what all producers do; I thought about how much we had left to do. Now the really hard part began—editing the final product. More than a year later on October 14, 1993, "Campaign for Cuba" aired nationally on PBS.

Sandra H. Dickson is an associate professor of broadcast journalism and political communication at the University of West Florida who has produced international news documentaries for PBS. Her work, "Campaign for Cuba," aired nationally on PBS in October 1992. She also has published articles in the areas of press criticism, political communication, and media ethics.

Is "Balanced" Coverage
Really Fair Coverage?

Robin K. Andersen

The nervous tension in the car hung hot and heavy, compounding the effects of the humid Salvadoran air. The car swung slowly through the winding streets of Lomas, the rich residential area on the outskirts of San Salvador. We slowed and began to turn into a driveway. The twelve-foot chainlink fence, woven with green plastic, concealed everything behind it. The gates opened slowly. As we maneuvered through, the guards came into view, at least half a dozen plainclothesmen armed with automatic rifles. It was too late to turn back. Kathy, the ABC correspondent, looked at me and said, "Wouldn't this make a good story? ABC News crew and graduate student kidnapped by the right-wing (paramilitary) in San Salvador."

It had not been my idea to come along. Yes, I was observing the newsgathering techniques of journalists covering Central America, and this was an important interview, but I knew it was going to be dangerous. The month before, Kathy had already been wounded by a bullet in the arm when the crew was covering a demonstration and she was hit by sniper fire. I had seen fear in their faces only yesterday after we had been separated at another demonstration. I had fallen back to interview one of the young organizers and had inadvertently put one of their pompoms in my pocket. When she saw me with it later, Kathy yelled, "Do you want to get killed?" Carl, the cameraman, added, "That makes a great target for right-wing snipers!" We knew these were dangerous people and so when the interview was arranged, I had said I would pass.

But here I was. We sat in the car for a few minutes not knowing what to do. The big double gates closed behind us, and the men in the lead car got out. John, the sound technician, was with them. We decided to get out too, and Carl slipped his camera from out of the trunk. John was

ahead carrying the rest of the gear. We walked along a garden path up to
the mansion and through the large, carved wooden doors. We were led
through the foyer, and as we entered a huge patio area we could see the
shimmering blue water of the swimming pool. As John proceeded to set
down the long cylindrical carrying case, one of the guards lurched forward and aimed his rifle. John's arms shot up over his head as he declared, "It's only a tripod!" He stood for a moment, looking like a character in a western who's just been told to *reach for the sky*. The armed man
finally gestured his approval, turning the gun away.

This freelance ABC News crew referred to themselves as the budget-
and-bang-bang crew. They flew into Central American "hot spots" after a
"coup or an earthquake" to get the pictures. It was February 1980, and El
Salvador had not yet become a major concern to the architects of U.S.
foreign policy. A year later the Reagan administration would "draw the
line against communist intervention in the hemisphere," and the high-
paid TV correspondents and network staff camera crews would take the
story.

But before El Salvador became famous, I watched as these freelancers,
with very few resources, struggled to comprehend what was going on in
the country. I wanted to know how U.S. journalists went about gathering
the news in a confusing and often dangerous situation. I had learned to
respect their intelligence and resourcefulness. Unlike their more highly
paid counterparts at the networks, these reporters understood Spanish.
We had driven through the streets of the capital listening to the radio. In
fact, the radio had helped us into the present situation. We heard a program featuring a speaker with such extreme right wing views that we knew
he had to be part of the story. Carl called the organization responsible
for the program and arranged an interview with Robert D'Aubuisson.
When we arrived at the office in a small shopping enclave in downtown
San Salvador, I said I would wait outside. But shortly after they went in,
they all came back out following several men. We were hurried into two
different cars, and as we drove off, I wondered if it had been a good idea
to leave our car there.

Now here we were, among armed men we knew to be dangerous, with
no car. As John began to set up the equipment on the patio, a small man
with curly black hair and large, sad, brown eyes emerged from one of the
rooms off the patio. His "handlers" ushered him over to the table and
instructed John how and where they wanted the interview done. As Kathy
began the interview with D'Aubuisson, I stepped aside, as was my habit,
and slowly struck up a conversation with two of the armed men guarding

the grounds from the swimming pool terrace. They told me they were pleased to have D'Aubuisson because he was so good on camera and had a "face that women loved." Through our rambling conversation they revealed their philosophy and plans for the country. They would eliminate the "communists" even if they had to kill 150,000 people. I learned that what they meant by "communist" was a huge proportion of the population that had taken to the streets demanding higher wages, fewer working hours, electricity in the countryside, and potable water.

I looked over to the men seated behind the table in front of the camera and realized that D'Aubuisson did not speak English. Kathy's questions were being answered by a tidy, pale, young man who, I later found out, had been educated in Boston. As the interview continued, the atmosphere lightened, and we all began to relax. After the last question, we declined to stay for drinks and asked for a ride back to our car. Under protest they agreed. On the way back they became excited about the idea of taking John and Carl up in a helicopter to view the crop damage caused by the war in the countryside. As they dropped us off, Carl said he would surely consider it.

Back at the hotel we let off much adrenaline as we each recounted our doubts and fears as the afternoon's events had played out. After a little while there was a knock on the door, and we all fell silent. Carl opened it, and one of the men from the mansion crowded into the small room. We acknowledged among ourselves through eye contact that he carried one of the typical wrist pouches that concealed a small revolver. He wanted to make arrangements for the helicopter trip, and he asked when the story would air on U.S. television. Carl told him that his work would not be complete until he finished the scheduled interview with the spokesperson for one of the largest popular organizations. Upon hearing this the man became agitated and gestured toward Carl yelling, "How can you talk to those people, they're communists!" Carl stood his ground, raised his hands in front of him, blocking the man's advance towards him, and said in a determined voice, "Hey, I tell both sides of the story."

Because I was not in the United States when the piece aired, it was over a year before I saw the ABC News story assembled from the videotape of the week's events. It bore so little resemblance to my experience that I hardly recognized it. Kathy and Carl were given one minute and thirty seconds to tell "both sides of the story." The ABC News report featured the *violence and extremism of both the left and right wing.* Telling "both sides of the story" had provided balance to a story that, in reality, had no balance. In El Salvador, the extremism of the left was hardly comparable to the activities of the right wing. This balanced story contradicted what the journalists themselves knew all too well—that the right wing paramilitary organizations were the dangerous ones. (During the early 1980s, tens of thousands of Salvadorans, mostly civilians, would be killed by the military and paramilitary organizations. News reports from the country would claim that the violence was caused by "extremism from both the right and the left," even though, as early as 1980, journalists knew that the right wing was responsible for the vast majority of the killings). One month after our interview with Robert D'Aubuisson, he and his organization would be implicated in the killing of the Monsignor Oscar Romero. Romero was assassinated after giving a sermon asking the military to throw down its weapons and stop the killing. D'Aubuisson would later come to be known as the "father of the death squads."

Telling both sides of the story is a professional canon promoted as a strategy to insure fairness and objectivity. Yet stories so often have many more sides than two. Conventional news narratives which present one view, then another, all too often fail to provide enough background information so that viewers can understand the situation and evaluate both claims from an informed perspective. The short denuded narratives of TV's "balanced" coverage of El Salvador could not explain the economic and political forces which were tearing the country apart. Most stories never mentioned how the armed civil insurrection was sparked in the first place. Background on the years of failed electoral struggle, military repression, and extreme conditions of poverty were not part of the exciting stories of violent demonstrations and political assassinations. The drama of violence and excitement was the primary news value of stories from El Salvador at that time. This was most clearly demonstrated to me by the "file footage" of a dead body tacked on at the end of Carl and Kathy's story, even though the "budget-and-bang-bang" crew had not filmed any deaths that week.

The false sense of balance often achieved by telling "two sides" of a story also provides a plausible narrative structure, allowing events to be pared down and fit into the highly abbreviated formats of broadcast journalism. But as Gaye Tuchman, author of *Making News: A Study in the Construction of Reality*, and W. Lance Bennett, author of *News: The Politics of Illusion*, have pointed out, the professional convention of telling "both sides of a story" can be understood, in one sense, as part of the "rituals of objectivity" whereby only the appearance of fairness is achieved.

I learned watching the process of journalism from beginning to end that "telling both sides of the story" is a journalistic convention that often obscures more than it illuminates. This was especially disturbing to me, given the dedication and conviction with which Carl had defended the practice, even in the face of danger.

Robin K. Andersen is chairwoman of the communications department at Fordham University. Her book Consumer Culture and Television Program-ming *was published by Westview Press in 1995, and her articles have appeared in books and scholarly journals such as* The Media Reader, Journalism and Popular Culture, Media Culture and Society, Latin American Perspectives, Social Text, EXTRA!, *and the* Humanist.

Power of the Press

Maurine H. Beasley

Years ago when I was a very green reporter for the *Kansas City Star,* I was the only reporter in the city room on a busy Saturday when a call came in to tell us that a group of Nobel Prize-winning scientists were at the airport between planes. (In those days—1959–1960— transcontinental planes stopped at Kansas City to refuel and passengers frequently changed aircraft.) No one else was available to interview them, which meant a huge leap forward for me from my usual task of writing a column listing awards received by Kansas City students.

I was terrified at the thought of talking to such distinguished individuals, since I knew nothing about their fields. The men were courteous and grave while I blundered around, having had absolutely no time to prepare myself for the assignment. Finally I asked if they ever worried about the ill effects of scientific discoveries, such as poison gas used in Nazi death camps. Their answer astounded me.

"Young lady," they said. "It's you who should worry about what you're doing. The communication of ideas is far more powerful than science. It's you, the journalists, who influence the way science is used—for good or for ill. Don't you forget it."

I never have.

Maurine H. Beasley holds bachelors' degrees in history and journalism from the University of Missouri/Columbia, a master's degree in journalism from Columbia University, and a Ph.D. in American studies from George Washington University. She is a former staff writer for the Kansas City Star *and the* Washington Post. *She is the author, coauthor, or editor of seven books dealing mainly with women and the media.*

About the Author

Retta Blaney has taught journalism at New York University, Brooklyn College, Marymount Manhattan College, and Montclair State University. She has worked as a reporter for newspapers in New York and Maryland, and her freelance articles have appeared in the *Washington Post, American Theater, Craine's New York Business,* and other publications. She holds an M.A. in modern drama from New York University, an M.F.A. in playwriting from Brooklyn College, and a B.A. in English from the College of Notre Dame of Maryland.